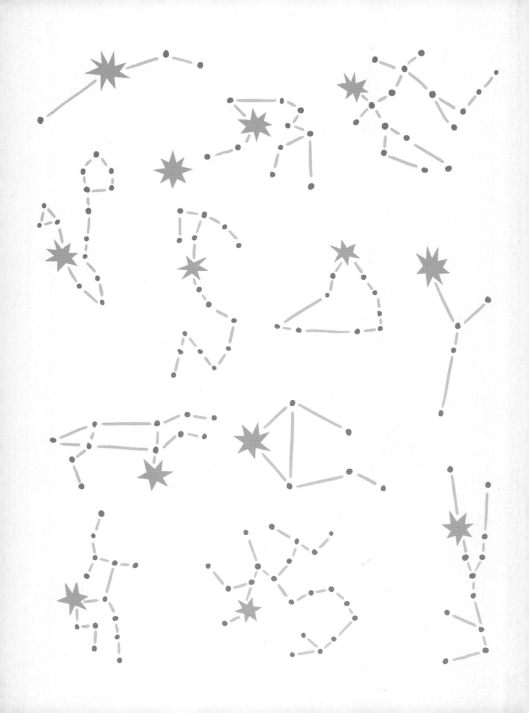

Written in Your Stars

Quarto.com

© 2025 Quarto Publishing Group USA Inc.
Text © 2025 Narayana Montúfar

First Published in 2025 by Fair Winds Press, an imprint of The Quarto Group,
100 Cummings Center, Suite 265-D, Beverly, MA 01915, USA.
T (978) 282-9590 F (978) 283-2742

Fair Winds Press titles are also available at discount for retail, wholesale, promotional, and bulk purchase. For details, contact the Special Sales Manager by email at specialsales@quarto.com or by mail at The Quarto Group, Attn: Special Sales Manager, 100 Cummings Center, Suite 265-D, Beverly, MA 01915, USA.

29 28 27 26 25   1 2 3 4 5

ISBN: 978-0-7603-9549-3

Digital edition published in 2025
eISBN: 978-0-7603-9550-9

Library of Congress Cataloging-in-Publication Data available.

Design: Cindy Samargia Laun
Cover image and illustrations: Caitlin Keegan, caitlinkeegan.com

Printed in China

The information in this book is for educational purposes only.
It is not intended to replace the advice of a physician or medical practitioner.
Please see your health-care provider before beginning any new health program.

Written in Your Stars

Use Your Saturn Return, Pluto
Square, and Other Planetary Cycles
to Become Your Best Self

NARAYANA MONTÚFAR

FAIR WINDS

CONTENTS

PART 3

Long-Term Planetary Cycles by Age

HARNESSING THE SLOW-MOVING PLANETS

PART 4

Short-Term Planetary Cycles

HARNESSING THE FASTEST PLANETS

INTRODUCTION

As one of the most ancient arts alive, astrology has many flavors, faces, and branches. Whether you want to predict specific events, find your soul's path, enhance your career and business, or improve your finances, there's a branch of astrology supporting that type of work. Astrology is as vast as the ocean and can be applied to many aspects of our lives.

Regardless of your astrological level of knowledge, you've most likely been exposed to the concept of "transits" as well as "horoscopes." Every time you see a social media post about "Mercury going retrograde" (the most well-known transit), and "how it will affect your sign" (your horoscope), you're being exposed to those two manifestations of astrology.

Written in Your Stars is quite different from the type of astrology you read in apps, magazines, or your favorite newsletters. This book is designed to help you become intimate with your own personal life cycles. Why cycles? A cycle is a series of events that regularly repeat in the same order. Astrologically speaking, these cycles are tied to the planets and mathematical points (a total of twelve) that reside in your birth chart. And guess what? They are predictable! The most important, life-changing cycles of your entire life are easy to pinpoint when searching for your current age, at any given time. If you ever desired to have a map to guide you in life as you age, this book can truly become your BFF!

By finding your current age in the "Timeline of Long-term Planetary Cycles by Age" (see page 44) and diving deep into the archetypes of the particular planet being highlighted, you will easily gain clarity around some of the themes that have recently been "taking over" your life. Not only will you figure out what is being asked of you, you will also get the chance to look back in time to see what was happening during an eventful time in your life. I highly recommend doing this—not to predict what will happen, but to re-examine and learn from your past reactions.

Besides receiving practical guidance that will take you from "coping" to "thriving" in these special moments, what this book intends is to create a sacred connection with all parts of yourself. Did you know that each of the ten planets floating in the solar system represents a different part of you? You are not just your Sun sign—you're so much more! You are a complex being with many layers, and this book is here to guide you in unraveling that deep and fascinating complexity. And because timing is everything, you will get closer to a specific planet whenever that planet is activated, which is something you can easily pinpoint just by knowing your age!

Now, to lay a strong foundation for the work we will do in this book, let's quickly look at what astrology is, how to approach it, and how to use it to your advantage.

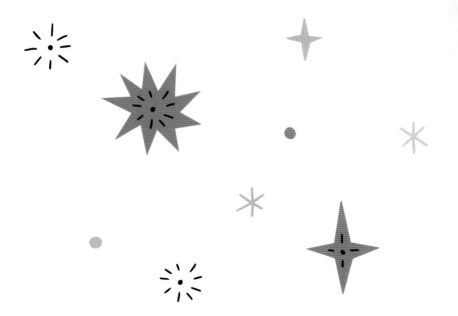

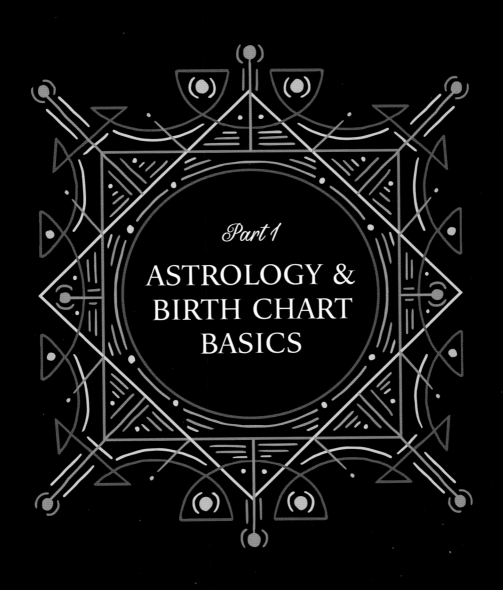

Part 1

ASTROLOGY &
BIRTH CHART
BASICS

WHAT IS ASTROLOGY?

When approaching the art of astrology, there are two common misconceptions we must clear up. The first one is that astrology is horoscopes, which is completely wrong. Horoscopes, based solely on the position of the Sun, are designed to bring astrology to the masses. While they sometimes resonate, they won't paint a full picture of what's happening to a given person at a very personal level.

The second misconception we debunk here is that astrology is mainly a predictive practice. Prediction can be a big part and focus of one's astrological practice. In fact, Horary Astrology, one of the very first branches of astrology, was born mainly as a predictive technique.

However, since our level of consciousness has evolved over time, we have grown into more humanistic and psychological ways of relating to the sky above us. This has driven us to realize that relying on prediction can sometimes prevent us from truly living in the moment. Prediction can also instigate a fear-based mentality, driving us to create self-fulfilling prophecies. Since relying on astrological prediction tends to deviate our energy from what's truly important, this is not the route this book is intended to take.

Simply put, astrology is the study of the movements and positions of the celestial bodies and how those influence human affairs and the natural world. It can be understood as the psychological application of astronomy, revealing countless details about a person's nature, strengths, weaknesses, and most importantly, their journey.

But above anything, astrology is a language of energy that studies the passage of time by exploring the meaning of planetary cycles. The word "cycles" refers to the circular planetary motion that all celestial bodies perform around the Sun, the star of our solar system. When analyzed from a big-picture perspective, these cycles reflect humanity's long-term collective behavior and path.

However, these cycles can also be studied from a personal perspective if we zoom into our birth chart to find meaning in our microcosmos. "Cycles" is a super important word to pay attention to, as what this book intends is to help you pinpoint your own cycles as a way to guide you through life.

THE POWER OF ASTROLOGY

In *Written in Your Stars,* we harness astrology in a more psychological fashion, always maneuvering life from a position of personal power in knowing that there is "free will." Instead of giving our power away to the planets and zodiac signs, we integrate them, work, and co-create with them! By studying their myth as well as their nature, we will travel back in time to determine how we have, so far, responded to their influence.

Then, whenever we are at a crossroads concerning our maneuvering of that same planet, we can catch ourselves and, if necessary, course-correct our responses. The power of astrology lies so much in creating awareness around our uniqueness, our actions, our desires, and our path.

Since astrology equals knowledge, and knowledge equals personal power, we must always operate from the perspective that our connection to astrology is sacred. The truth is that, without even knowing, you have already established a relationship with astrology since the day you were born. *Written in Your Stars* guides you in becoming aware of the nature of that relationship. Like I always say to my clients, truly diving into the ancient art of astrology is like experiencing the most fascinating love story. It comes with ups and downs, inner dramas, infatuations, major epiphanies, and moments of pure ecstasy!

Are you ready?

You are now being put face-to-face with astrology, with your entire awareness—because *you are ready*! The reason why you are here with me is because your soul and spirit desire to unravel the gifts your astral DNA has for you. And as you will soon see, if you truly allow yourself to dive into this art, there rarely is a way back. Once you begin unlocking the gifts that were written in your stars at your moment of birth, you will see life for what it is: an opportunity to learn, grow, and thrive.

YOUR BIRTH CHART

When working with astrology, it's impossible not to run into the concept of natal charts. Also known as a birth chart, a natal chart is a snapshot of the exact position of the planets at your exact moment of birth. This snapshot captures an infinite number of things about you—your very first breath, as well as the archetypes that will be present in your life.

If you are reading this book, you most likely already know certain aspects of your chart. If you don't, don't fret. You are, for sure, in for some epiphanies as we will be working with specific planetary activations that everyone experiences at the same age. That being said, the more intimate you become with your birth chart, the more you will get out of this book. And for that to happen, you might want to consider getting a reading with a professional astrologer so they walk you through it. Getting a professional reading will function as your seed moment, taking you on a blooming journey full of sweetness, intense epiphanies, and life-changing realizations that can only develop over time.

If you do not know your birth chart yet . . . welcome! This book will truly give you a strong foundation when it comes to understanding it. Put special attention to the upcoming section: Your Birth Chart as a Movie, as it will help you understand, in simple terms, how astrology works.

To clear out a lot of doubts or misconceptions about birth charts, below are some helpful points to remember at any time during your upcoming astro-journey.

BIRTH CHART FACTS

Birth Chart Fact #1: You have all ten planets and all twelve zodiac signs in your birth chart! Let's begin by remembering that when it comes to astrological interpretation, we are not just our Sun sign. The ten planets that exist in our solar system are in each one of our charts, with each planet representing a specific part of ourselves. Similarly, the twelve zodiac signs you know are all inside your chart, too. You are not just "a Taurus" or just "a Scorpio." Both Taurus and Scorpio are somewhere in your chart and mean something to you. More on that later— but for now, let that thought just sink in: *You have all ten planets and all twelve zodiac signs in your birth chart!*

Birth Chart Fact #2: Your birth chart truly is unique to you! Perhaps the most fascinating aspect of diving into astrology is realizing that your astrological experience is incomparable. Take the ten planets and the twelve signs and randomly put them together—you can get about 120 different combinations! To illustrate this fact, let's put it this way: Even twins born seconds apart are not going to have the same life journey. The reason is that there are multiple ways in which planets can manifest, plus another world of human ways in which we each respond to them. This is when the universal law of "free will" comes into play. More likely than not, even twins, consciously or unconsciously, respond differently to a shared planet-sign combination.

Birth Chart Fact #3: You're not going to feel your entire chart all at once. Just like it happens in a movie, when not all of the actors appear on the screen at the same time, the planets inside a birth chart also take their turns in the spotlight. Different planets get highlighted during different times—some for just a few days, some for weeks, some for months, and some for years! For this reason, it's key to know which planets have been awakened by your current age, making this a great time to create awareness around the relationship you have established with that specific planet.

Birth Chart Fact #4: You don't have to be an astrologer to know and work with your chart. While many astrology fanatics decide to leap into reading other people's charts, doing so is not a requirement for this type of work to be meaningful. If you're here for more personal development than astrology, focusing on analyzing your own cycles will help you stay focused and get deeper into the process. After all, astrology is an amazing tool for understanding ourselves and how we interact with our environment.

YOUR BIRTH CHART AS A MOVIE

This section will be very useful if you are new to the art of astrology or you have been looking at your birth chart as a list. Birth charts are organically round and should be analyzed this way from the very beginning of our self-study journey. Like the Sun, the Moon, our very own Earth, and all the planets in our solar system, birth charts are round, relating to the energetic symbol of the circle, which means infinity.

When we first see a birth chart and all its moving parts, our minds automatically get visually challenged—it's a lot! However, the more times we see it, the better we will understand it. Of course, learning the planetary symbols as well as the zodiac sign symbols is the first step, as they are the foundations of this language.

An analogy that has been incredibly helpful for me when reading for a first-time client is comparing the birth chart to a movie. This comparison works well, as it takes into consideration all the moving pieces, as well as the fact that every chart is unique. Let's look at it!

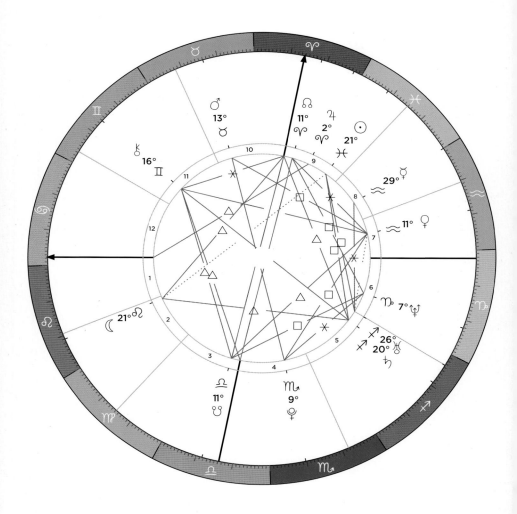

Birth Chart Example
Mar 12, 1987
2:33:00 PM GMT-7
Lat 34° N 03' 12.0"
Lng 118° W 14' 32.0"
Placidus
Tropical
Geocentric

The Planets as Actors

In your birth chart movie, the symbols inside the white spaces are the planets, which are the most important part of the movie taking place. If you don't have the actors, you don't have a movie, even if you have the most amazingly written script. This is a fantastic opportunity to reiterate that the most important aspect of a birth chart is not the zodiac signs. Each one of the symbols (the planets you see), is within your chart and represents a different part of you—that is how colorful and complex you are!

The Zodiac Signs as Costumes

Secondary are the zodiac signs, which in this case function as the costumes the actors wear. For example, the Moon—which in astrology rules our emotions, our private selves, and subconscious patterns—adopts a very different flavor in each of the zodiac signs. The Moon is still the Moon in its nature whether it is located in Leo or Scorpio. In Leo, it will be loud and dramatic, and in Scorpio, it will be intense and reserved when it comes to expressing emotions.

An important concept to delineate here is that each planet likes and dislikes certain costumes—yes, there is favoritism in astrology! This is what helps astrologers gauge a person's strengths and weaknesses, actually. A planet that is in a costume (zodiac sign) that it feels comfortable in will have an easier time performing its role. And a planet that is not dressed in a costume to its liking will have a harder time doing its job and will require more of your attention. While some astrologers disagree with this concept of "planetary favoritism," after reading for hundreds of individuals, I have seen it in work over and over again. You will see this concept developing more deeply as the book progresses.

The Astrological Houses as the Movie Sets

Lastly, we have the movie sets, which are the twelve white spaces numbered from 1 to 12, which is where the actors are performing. These are called "houses" and each represents a different part of your life. If you have an empty house in your birth chart—which you most likely do—that doesn't mean you don't have that part of life, as each house is still ruled by a specific planet.

Below is what each astrological house represents:
- 1st house: identity, self-image, the body, approach to life
- 2nd house: money, resources, budget, personal values
- 3rd house: speech, communication, siblings, transportation
- 4th house: home, family, roots, foundations
- 5th house: children, fun, play, romance, creativity
- 6th house: work, wellness, pets, life processes
- 7th house: relationships, marriage, contracts, business partners
- 8th house: healing sex, intimacy, transformation, your partner's money
- 9th house: travel, learning, spirituality, life philosophy
- 10th house: career, reputation, visibility, life purpose
- 11th house: community, friendships, networking, hopes and dreams
- 12th house: spirituality, healing, secrets, the subconscious mind

The Astrological Aspects as the Movie Script

The third layer is the astrological aspects, which are the colorful lines you see between the planets. These are the conversations the planets have, functioning as the movie script. The blue lines are "positive or easy conversations" and the red and green are "challenging conversations" between the actors. The planets (actors) that share blue lines will work with and help one another, and the planets that share a red line have some sort of drama that will need to be resolved during the movie.

Now, let's look at two examples of how this movie analogy works by quickly examining the birth charts of a couple of well-known individuals.

At right is the birth chart of Nikola Tesla, the brilliant nineteenth-century Serbian-American inventor and engineer who pioneered many of the electrical systems and processes that are still in use today in radio, television, and machinery. Nikola was a Cancer Sun, Libra Moon, and Taurus Rising. However, the planet we must highlight is Uranus, being the defining force in both chart and overall life. In Nikola's chart, Uranus is in Taurus in the First House.

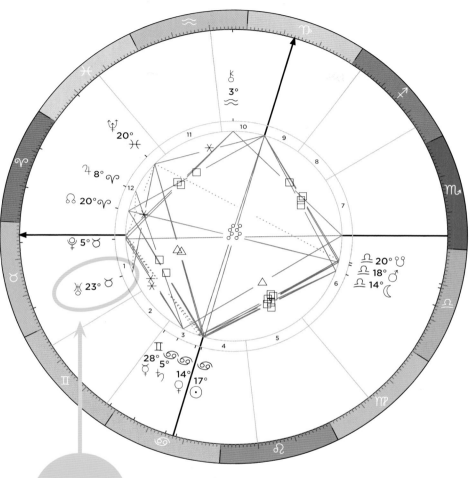

Uranus in
Taurus in the
First House

Nikola Tesla
Jul 10, 1856
12:00:00 AM GMT+1
Gospić 09
Lat 44° N 33′ 8.2″
Lng 15° E 22′ 36.8″
Placidus
Tropical
Geocentric

Let's pull this placement apart following the movie analogy:

The Actor: Uranus
Uranus is the planet of innovation, electricity, scientific invention, freedom, originality, and the future.

The Costume: Taurus
Taurus is the first earth sign of the zodiac, strongly connected to beauty, money, material resources, and personal values.

The Movie Set: The First House
The first house is the house of self, identity, appearance, and consciousness. Any planet in this house will highly color how the outside environment will see that individual.

Nikola Tesla was perceived as a loner and eccentric genius with extremely sensible capabilities who disliked interacting with people but deeply loved helping society at large. Handsome, magnetic, and elegant (Taurus Rising), Nikola never married due to his need for "freedom" to continue working on his groundbreaking inventions. Due to his technological discoveries (Uranus), he became a millionaire (Taurus) before the age of forty, but gave most of his money to charity.

One of his most well-known quotes—"If you want to understand the universe, think of energy, frequency, and vibration"—seemed outer worldly at the time, and no one would deny he was ahead of his time! Between May 1899 and 1900, while he had a laboratory in Colorado Springs, he claimed to have received signals from another planet. Uranus also happens to rule all things alien!

As you can see, while there's a lot more to unpack about his birth chart, Uranus was the main actor in Nikola Tesla's movie!

Now let's look at the chart of Alexandria Ocasio-Cortez (see page 22), the left-wing American politician who, during her Saturn Return, became the youngest woman ever to serve in the United States Congress. And whether you agree with her views or not, you can't deny she is a force on a quest to "tax the rich."

Alexandria is a Sagittarius Rising, with a Libra Sun and an Aries Moon. We will bring attention to both of her luminaries: her Sun in Libra in the Tenth House, and her Moon in Aries in the Third House.

This is what happens when analyzing these two placements via the movie analogy:

The Actor: The Sun

Astrologically, the Sun is the light that shines on the world, relating to our ego and the parts of our personality of which we are conscious.

The Costume: Libra

Alexandria's Libra Sun is the perfect example of someone who is deeply concerned with justice, illuminating all the imbalances within her country's complex politics.

The Movie Set: The Tenth House

Out of all twelve houses in the birth chart, this is the one that rules our career inclinations as well as the role we play in society.

The Movie Script: Sun conjunct Mars

Alexandria's Sun is sitting next to Mars, the planet of drive, ambition, and masculine energy. In her movie, the Sun and Mars are "pals," "working together" for a specific purpose, which is to bring justice (Libra) to society (Tenth House) as activism is her calling.

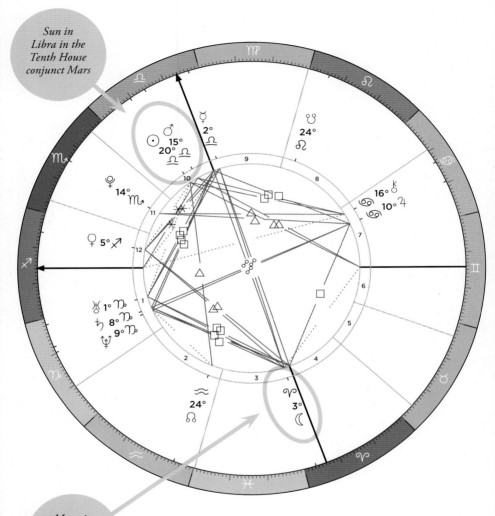

Sun in Libra in the Tenth House conjunct Mars

Moon in Aries in the Third House square Saturn

Alexandria Ocasio-Cortez
Oct 13, 1989
11:50:00 AM GMT-4
New York NY
Lat 40° N 42' 46.7"
Lng 74° W 00' 25.9"
Placidus
Tropical
Geocentric

Let's also look at her Moon placement:

The Actor: The Moon
If the Sun is the conscious part of ourselves, the Moon is the subconscious layer of our being. Our Moon sign depicts how we express emotions and the "true driver" behind our actions.

The Costume: Aries
As the first fire sign of the zodiac, Aries is unapologetic and goes for the gold. With an infinite amount of energy, any planet in Aries will chase its desires with incredible amounts of stamina.

The Movie Set: The Third House
This is the house of communication, speech, intellect, and community work.

The Movie Script: Moon square Saturn
The Moon (emotions and survival instincts) are clashing with Saturn (tradition, the establishment).

Alexandria's Moon in Aries in the Third House makes her a passionate and unapologetic communicator, as the Third House is the absolute best astrological house for the Moon to be in! Even in front of the biggest audiences, she dares to say what others would be frightened of even mentioning. Aries-style, she is not afraid of ruffling any feathers, as in the end, she is speaking "the truth." During her campaigning, her speeches are delivered with full-on honesty, making her easily relatable. Lastly, the Moon-Saturn square in her chart (the script, or conversation between planets) tells us that besides taxing the rich, she's also on a quest to unseat the patriarchy!

What are the actors, costumes, sets, and scripts of your movie? This would be the perfect time to find out and start getting acquainted with them, as discovering them will play a big role when working with your astrological cycles.

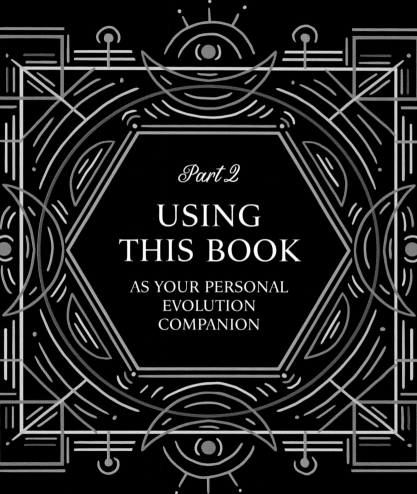

Part 2

USING
THIS BOOK

AS YOUR PERSONAL
EVOLUTION
COMPANION

FINDING YOUR PERSONAL CYCLES

Unlike most astrology books, *Written in Your Stars* doesn't begin by educating the reader about the basics of astrology, per se—although you might naturally absorb some information about the planets and their effect on your life.

This is also a good opportunity to differentiate planetary cycles from *transits*, which is a similar technique that astrologers use to figure out what a person is experiencing through their chart at any given moment. When astrologers look at a client's transits, the possibilities are endless, as we're dealing with the connections the ten traveling planets in the sky are forming with the ten planets in a person's chart. If you do the math, there are 144 possibilities—and that is without taking into consideration asteroids and mathematical points! An example of a transit is: Transiting Pluto squaring natal Moon, transiting Uranus conjunct natal Mars, or transiting Neptune sextile natal Sun.

Written in Your Stars is different in the sense that it only deals with the connections between the same planet. For example, Transiting Uranus square natal Uranus, transiting Neptune sextile natal Neptune—and of course, includes the unforgettable Saturn Return, which technically happens when transiting Saturn is conjunct your natal Saturn.

This book is designed to give you, the reader, context and guidance regarding your planetary cycles so you can both prepare for the future and go back in time so you can zoom into the themes that a specific planet carries for you. We all have a special and specific relationship with each one of the planets in our solar system. *Written in Your Stars* will assist you in unveiling the magical connection you have with each one of them! For this reason, this book is structured in a way that facilitates an intimate connection with the planet(s) that currently requests attention or awareness.

For example, as I begin writing this book, I am forty-three years old. Therefore, in the Timeline of Predictable Cycles, I am right in between my Jupiter Opposition (age forty-two) and my second Saturn Opposition (age forty-four). As I sit in this liminal space between two cycles of opposing nature (Jupiter: growth vs. Saturn: contraction), my mental focus should be on transitioning from Jupiter to Saturn.

What transpired for me last year, and how does that relate to the themes that will come up for me next year? As you will notice when reading the Jupiter chapter in this book, Jupiter is benevolent, which means that is one of the "easiest" planets to master. However, like everything in life and every planet in astrology, Jupiter also has a "shadow side," and I'm not afraid to admit I experienced it in 2022. Due to Jupiter being of an optimistic nature, this planet can sometimes make us feel "magnanimous and invincible."

At that time, I had just experienced success in my astrological career due to the 2021 release of my first book, *Moon Signs: Unluck Your Inner Luminary Power*. I felt really good about myself and my capabilities and in 2022, I definitely bit off way more than what I could chew at the time. I found myself spread too thin, tired, and in the end . . . defeated. I entered an art contest in which I invested a lot of time, money, and energy—and didn't win the competition after feeling very confident that the art piece I had created for the contest would win. Clearly, I survived, but it took me a while to regain my confidence in my artistic skills.

Now, as I head into my second Saturn Opposition next year, it is crucial that I begin working with this actor in my movie, as well as how it is placed in my chart, so I can handle this moment feeling prepared and ready. Since Jupiter *expands* and Saturn *contracts*, my current learning is that, in order to truly succeed, I must invest my time and energy only in the projects that truly matter. I can't do it all, and overextending myself sets me up for failure.

The phrase "history repeats itself" applies to everything, even the ancient art of astrology. In this next personal example, what I am doing is looking back to what transpired for me when I was fourteen years old, when I experienced my First Saturn Opposition. At that time, my life changed tremendously, so it is quite easy for me to pinpoint my "Saturnian" story.

At age thirteen, I was living with my mom in a little fishing village on Mexico's Pacific coast, Zihuatanejo. I was having an absolute blast living by the beach, running around, and playing with my friends. I was attending the best private school in town; however, the overall level of education wasn't that high there. My mom was traveling and left me at my friend's home under her family's watch. This is when Master Teacher Saturn comes in! As you will see in the Saturn section, this planet often comes in the form of a teacher, an authority figure, or an elder.

When my grandparents found out my mom had gone on a trip and left me with my friend's family, they immediately got on a plane to Zihuatanejo and convinced me to come to live with them in Mexico City. I took the bait! They promised me they would put me in the country's best schools and they did. However, since my education level was below the best schools in Mexico, I spent my entire year (fourteen), studying with a private teacher, even after school and on weekends, so I could level up to the school my grandparents aspired me to attend. Looking back, it was one of the hardest years of my life, but without it, I would probably not be writing this book. That school is where I learned how to write clearly and properly.

Next year, when I turn forty-four, I will not have Saturn show up exactly as I did when I was fourteen. My amazing grandparents, Jorge and Patricia, have passed, but Saturn could come in the form of another authority figure whose entrance into my life will teach me something I need to experience. I can also foresee that it will be a year of tremendous learning in the form of personal development.

In addition to mapping our futures, studying our personal astrological cycles can inspire us to honor our past.

Within our personal evolution, the planetary activations and cycles are (mostly all) predictable and are here to level us up, constantly sustaining and elevating our process of self-actualization. My hope is that you use this book as your personal companion, honoring the past experiences that made you who you are, while helping you co-create your life with the influence of your planets, the actors of your movie. And in this movie, you are the director—never forget that!

IDENTIFYING THE TWO DIFFERENT TYPES OF PLANETARY CYCLES

We have arrived at that part of the book in which we begin analyzing your planetary cycles—which is exciting! To do that, we must get into the nitty-gritty of how the planets move in the sky and the relationship they form with the planets in your chart.

We will study the cycles of all twelve planetary influences pertaining to their position in each of our birth charts. In astrology, our relationship with a specific planet (actor within our movie) is defined by the zodiac sign (costume) and astrological house (movie set) that planet was occupying at our exact moment of birth. In this case, this planet's position is static, it doesn't move, as what our birth charts do is freeze the position of the planet by capturing the sky at the moment of birth. When we refer to the "planet's cycle," we will be referring to the relationship that *the same transiting or moving planet* has at specific times with the planet in your chart.

In the graphic on page 30, transiting Jupiter in Leo is forming a trine with the natal chart Jupiter, which is in Aries. The Jupiter in Aries placement in the natal chart is static, while transiting Jupiter will keep moving further into Leo, then Virgo, then Libra, and so on.

As you will see further in the book, the type of planetary movement (fast or slow) is important, and the reason why they have been separated into two different chapters.

The planetary cycles that involve slowing-moving planets happen less frequently and will last for longer periods. One could see these slow-moving, long-term planetary cycles as "visitors" who come over and stay with us for months, changing our overall routine and life experience.

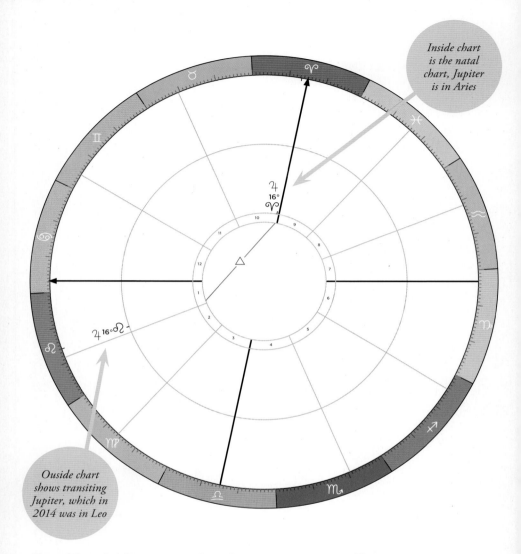

Inside chart is the natal chart, Jupiter is in Aries

Ouside chart shows transiting Jupiter, which in 2014 was in Leo

Transiting Jupiter to Natal Jupiter
Apr 24, 1999
11:39:00 AM GMT-7
Lat 34° N 03' 12.0"
Lng 118° W 14' 32.0"
Placidus
Tropical
Geocentric

Now
Oct 01, 2014
10:52:19 AM PDT
Lat 37° N 48' 17.0"
Lng 122° W 16' 21.0"
Placidus
Tropical
Geocentric

Since the planetary cycles that involve faster-moving planets happen more often, they are quicker and tend to create less impact. One could see these fast planets as "visitors" who come over and stay with us for only a few nights. However, they still matter, as the faster-moving cycles may function as triggers for the slow-moving cycles.

While this concept could be a little hard to understand at first, once it is fully digested, it will blow your mind when it comes to understanding not only how astrology works but how our personal cycles work.

Let's take Mars as an example. As you will see below, Mars takes two years to make a circle around the Sun, so that means we all get our "Mars Return" every two years. During this planetary cycle, Martian themes (masculine energy, ambition, anger, sexual drive) return to be "revisited." However, within those two years, there will be three more times in which we will greatly experience *transiting Mars* activating *natal Mars*.

For example, I was born with Mars at 25 degrees of Leo, which is one of the most intense astrological forces in my chart. Mars in Leo is creative, bold, and ambitious—but can also be quite impulsive and explosive when it doesn't get its way. The next time I feel Mars in this cycle is when Mars (while traveling in the sky) reaches 25 degrees Scorpio; the third time is when Mars reaches 25 degrees of Aquarius; and then finally, when Mars reaches 25 degrees of Taurus. Since Mars rules drive, it's an important planetary cycle, as this entire tour in the sky will denote how I chase my goals. However, due to Mars being one of the fastest-moving planets, this planetary cycle repeats quite often, every two years.

Planetary cycles involving slower-moving planets last longer, repeat less, and become more important. The best example: Saturn's cycle is thirty years and, therefore, its effects are quite massive—who hasn't heard of the infamous Saturn Return? It's not that the cycles of faster-moving planets don't matter—they do, but because they are very different in nature and also calculation, we will divide the twelve planetary influences into two categories: Faster Cycles (short-term) and Slower Cycles (long-term).

PLANETARY SPEED AND MOVEMENT

Slower Cycles

The slower-moving planets are a more similar variable in the charts of people around you. When comparing your chart to the charts of your friends, you will most likely have the same Chiron, Uranus, Neptune, and Pluto signs. Because these planetary bodies move extremely slowly, they span entire generations—and, therefore, are also called "generational planets." For this reason, the planetary cycles involving these planetary bodies are easier to predict by the age factor.

- **Jupiter** represents your power of attraction, your luck, and your philosophy of life. *Cycle: Jupiter takes twelve years to circle the entire zodiac.*
- **Saturn** represents your sense of responsibility, how you build a legacy, and where you become a master. *Cycle: Saturn takes thirty years to circle the entire zodiac.*
- **Chiron** represents your sore spot, how you must seek healing and turn deep wounds into personal power. *Cycle: Chiron takes fifty to fifty-one years to circle the entire zodiac.*
- **Uranus** represents your ability to change, how you seek freedom, and how you express authenticity. *Cycle: Uranus takes eighty-four years to circle the entire zodiac.*
- **Neptune** represents your imagination, spirituality, cultural inclinations, and your blind spots. *Cycle: Neptune takes one hundred and sixty-five years to circle the entire zodiac.*
- **Pluto** represents your ability to rise above challenges and overcome trauma. *Cycle: Pluto takes two hundred and forty-eight years to circle the entire zodiac.*
- **The Lunar Nodes of Destiny** relate to your soul's journey, helping you integrate the learnings from your past lives so you can integrate them into your focus for this incarnation. *Cycle: The Lunar Nodes take eighteen years to circle the entire zodiac.*

Faster Cycles

Due to the following planets moving so fast, they are a much more different variable in natal charts. For example, your Venus and Mercury signs will most likely differ greatly from person to person. If you check the charts of your friends and family, they will most likely have Venus or Mercury in a different sign than you. For this reason, it's hard to calculate these short-term, faster planetary cycles. As you will see in the next chapters:

- **The Moon** represents your emotions, inner life, subconscious patterns, and who you really are. This is the reason why there is a New Moon and a Full Moon once every single month. *Cycle: The Moon takes one month to circle the entire zodiac.*
- **The Sun** represents your ego, your identity, and the light you came to shine on the world. Astrologically speaking, this cycle is the reason why you have your birthday once a year, which is called your Solar Return. *Cycle: The Sun takes one year to circle the entire zodiac.*
- **Mercury** represents how you think, write, communicate, and process information. *Cycle: Mercury takes one year to circle the entire zodiac.*
- **Venus** represents what you are attracted to, what you like and dislike, and your love language. *Cycle: Venus takes one year to circle the entire zodiac.*
- **Mars** represents how you go after your anger, your sex drive, and how you chase your goals. *Cycle: Mars takes two years to circle the entire zodiac.*

As you can see, planetary cycles differ greatly, which is quite an important concept to grasp. Paying attention to this *speed* is crucial when figuring out when our next "encounter" is with each planet as well as its influence and archetypes. The nature of these types of encounters will depend on the nature of the "aspect" the transiting planet forms with the natal planet. Remember, within our movie analogy, the "aspects" function as the "script" between the actors—so let's look at them.

ASPECTS: UNDERSTANDING HOW
PLANETARY MOVEMENT AFFECTS US

When it comes to understanding how astrology works, analyzing the astrological aspects is crucial. Astrological aspects can be understood as the conversations the planets are having with one another. These "conversations" or "scripts" are based on mathematical angles and can either be positive (easy) or negative (hard).

Simply put, "aspects" refer to the angles the planets create in any given astrological chart. However, in this book, we will mainly study the conversation a "transiting planet is having with a natal planet." In our previous example of Jupiter, we would focus on the conversation transiting Jupiter in Scorpio is having with the natal Jupiter in Pisces, for example.

While mathematical calculations create many astrological aspects, there are five main astrological aspects: the conjunction, the opposition, the square, the trine, and the sextile.

Conjunction: In astrology, the most potent aspect is the conjunction, when planets are 0 degrees apart. Within our study, a conjunction happens when we experience a planetary return; when a planet traveling in the sky returns to the exact position it was in when we were born. At right is an example of a Venus return, which in this case, happens in the zodiac sign of Taurus.

Conjunction

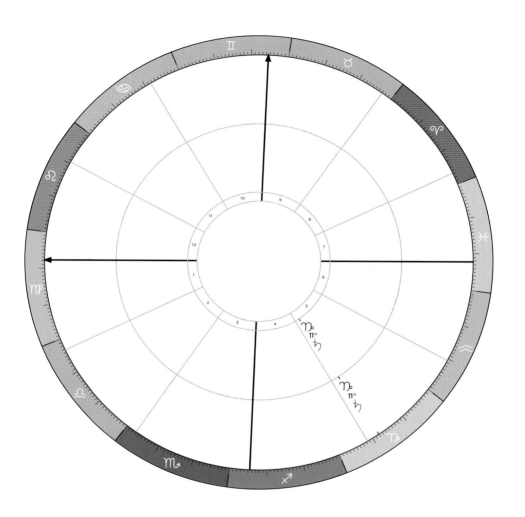

Conjunction Example
Jun 13, 1989
11:39:00 AM GMT-7
Lat 34° N 03' 12.0"
Lng 118° W 14' 32.0"
Placidus
Tropical
Geocentric

Now
Jan 03, 2019
10:10:40 AM PST
Lat 37° N 48' 17.0"
Lng 122° W 16' 21.0"
Placidus
Tropical
Geocentric

Hard Aspects

After conjunctions, the most potent aspects are called hard aspects, which are considered the most difficult to maneuver. However, hard aspects are also useful, as they create the tension and energy required to keep us moving! Hard aspects bring an "I have to do something" type of energy—a conversation or an action must happen.

Opposition: An opposition occurs when two planets are 180 degrees apart, as far away as they can be, occupying opposite signs of the zodiac. This is an epic clash between the transiting planet and the natal planet. Oppositions pull the energies in two different directions, which requires a balancing act and integration of two polar energies. At right is an example of a Mars-Mars opposition return, which in this case, happens when transiting Mars in Aquarius sits exactly across from natal Mars in Leo.

Square: A square occurs when two planets are 90 degrees apart, creating tension between the two planets involved. Squares create moments of "crisis," but sometimes, a crisis is necessary to stimulate action. While squares bring stress and obstacles, they represent the big lessons we need in order to grow. On page 38 is an example of a transiting Saturn (in Aquarius) forming a square with natal Saturn (in Taurus), which is one of the most journeys in one's lifetime.

Both oppositions and squares are aspects that demand "action." The main difference between an opposition and a square is that the opposition occurs in zodiac signs whose elements are compatible. Squares can only happen between planets that are in zodiac signs whose elements are completely incompatible.

Opposition

Square

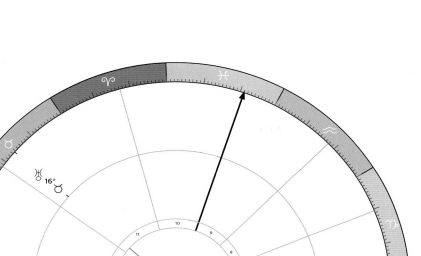

Opposition Example
Jul 23, 1979
3:33:00 AM GMT-7
Lat 34° N 03' 12.0"
Lng 118° W 14' 32.0"
Placidus
Tropical
Geocentric

Now
Jun 01, 2022
11:13:50 AM PDT
Lat 37° N 48' 17.0"
Lng 122° W 16' 21.0"
Placidus
Tropical
Geocentric

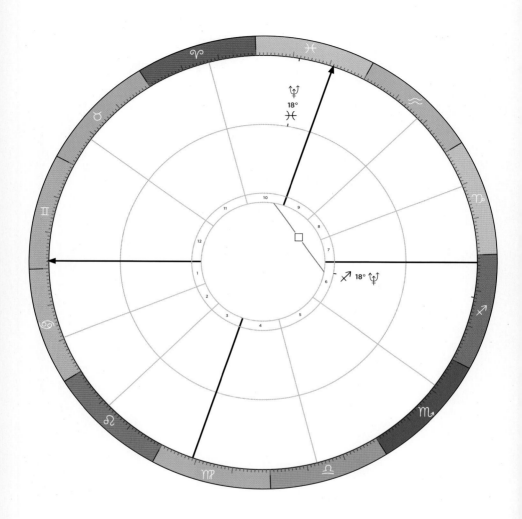

Square Example
Jul 23, 1979
3:33:00 AM GMT-7
Lat 34° N 03' 12.0"
Lng 118° W 14' 32.0"
Placidus
Tropical
Geocentric

Now
Dec 18, 2020
10:16:14 AM PST
Lat 37° N 48' 17.0"
Lng 122° W 16' 21.0"
Placidus
Tropical
Geocentric

Easy Aspects

The easy aspects are the trine and the sextile, and as their name implies, they are the easiest aspects to maneuver. However, easy aspects lack the energy to inspire or create change or action. For this reason, we sometimes don't even notice them, and we miss out on harnessing their influence if not aware of them.

Trine: A trine occurs when two planets are 120 degrees apart, creating harmony and a flow of energy between the two. Things come easily and happen naturally with the trine, which can sometimes create complacency and subconscious responses. For this reason, trines can also be tricky if we are not aware of the opportunities they can bring us. On page 40 is an example of the transiting Sun in Pisces forming a trine with the natal Sun in Scorpio.

Sextile: A sextile occurs when two planets are 60 degrees apart, creating cooperation between the two planets involved. Like the trine, it creates an easy flow of energy, except that the planets are closer together from one another, which means that sooner rather than later, they will be conjunct, in the case that it is a slower-moving planet. On page 41 is an example of transiting Uranus in Aries forming a sextile with natal Uranus in Aquarius.

Both trines and sextiles are aspects of "ease" and "flow." The difference between trines and sextiles is that the sextile is more noticeable to us, as the planets involved really want to cooperate with one another. For this reason, we are more likely to notice sextiles at a conscious level—and, therefore, to channel their energy more constructively.

If this concept of "aspects" is too hard to understand now, don't let it scare you. In the next chapters, during which we will review each planet, you will be able to easily pinpoint what type of aspect you are experiencing just by finding your current age.

Trine

Sextile

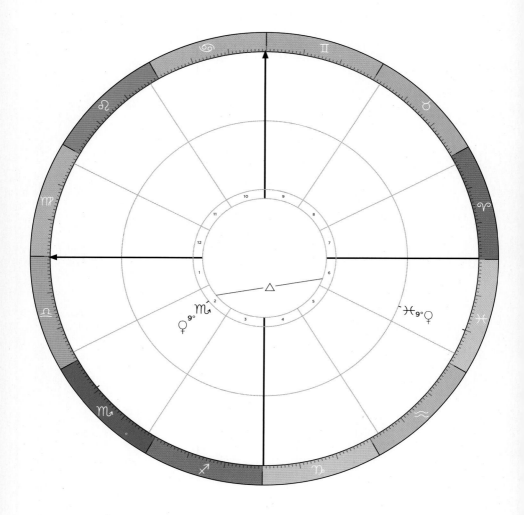

Trine Example
Nov 11, 1986
3:33:00 AM GMT-7
Lat 34° N 03' 12.0"
Lng 118° W 14' 32.0"
Placidus
Tropical
Geocentric

Now
Jan 12, 2025
10:18:00 AM PST
Lat 37° N 48' 17.0"
Lng 122° W 16' 21.0"
Placidus
Tropical
Geocentric

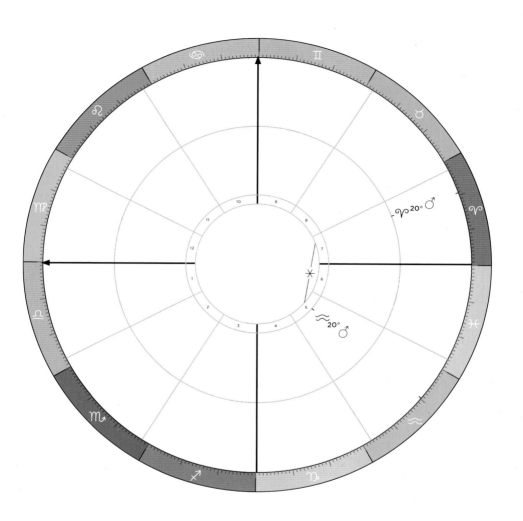

Sextile Example
Nov 11, 1986
3:33:00 AM GMT-7
Lat 34° N 03' 12.0"
Lng 118° W 14' 32.0"
Placidus
Tropical
Geocentric

Now
May 27, 2024
11:22:16 AM PDT
Lat 37° N 48' 17.0"
Lng 122° W 16' 21.0"
Placidus
Tropical
Geocentric

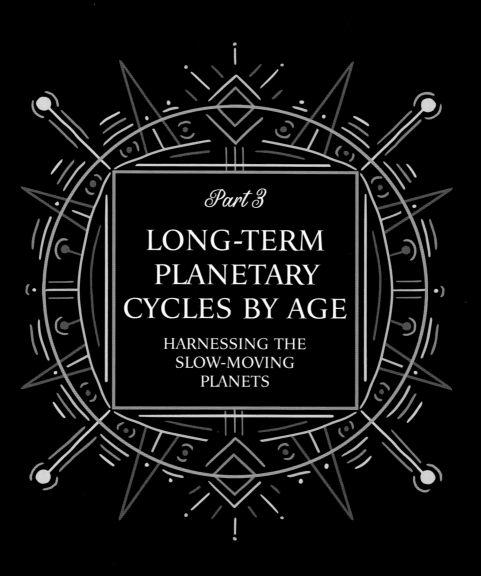

Part 3

LONG-TERM PLANETARY CYCLES BY AGE

HARNESSING THE SLOW-MOVING PLANETS

TIMELINE OF LONG-TERM PLANETARY CYCLES BY AGE

These are approximate ages to make it easy to visualize which planets and cycles are being activated throughout your life. To find the exact dates, visit the calculator created for *Written in Your Stars*: www.naramon.com/written-in-your-stars-calculator.

Age	1	2	3	4	5	6	7	8	9	10	11	12	13	14	15	16	17	18	19	20
Jupiter		■	■	■		■	■		■			■			■			■	■	
Saturn				■			■								■			■		
Uranus														■	■					
Neptune																		■		
Lunar Nodes		■	■			■	■					■	■				■	■		
Pluto Sextile																				
Pluto Square																				
Pluto Trine																				
Pluto Opposition																				
Chiron Return																				
Chiron Sextile			■	■	■	■	■	■	■	■	■	■	■	■	■	■	■	■	■	■
Chiron Square						■	■	■	■	■	■	■	■	■	■	■	■	■	■	■
Chiron Waxing Trine																				
Chiron Waning Trine																				
Chiron Opposition													■	■	■	■	■	■	■	■

Age	51	52	53	54	55	56	57	58	59	60	61	62	63	64	65	66	67	68	69	70
Jupiter	■	■		■	■		■	■		■			■	■		■	■		■	■
Saturn		■	■				■			■			■			■			■	■
Uranus																			■	■
Neptune																		■		
Lunar Nodes	■			■	■					■	■					■	■		■	■
Pluto Sextile																				
Pluto Square	■	■	■	■	■	■	■	■	■	■										
Pluto Trine	■	■																		
Pluto Opposition																				
Chiron Return																				
Chiron Sextile																				
Chiron Square													■	■	■	■	■	■	■	■
Chiron Waxing Trine																				
Chiron Waning Trine																				
Chiron Opposition													■	■	■	■	■	■	■	■

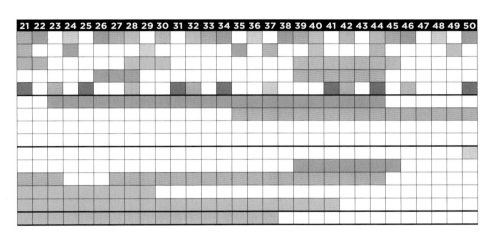

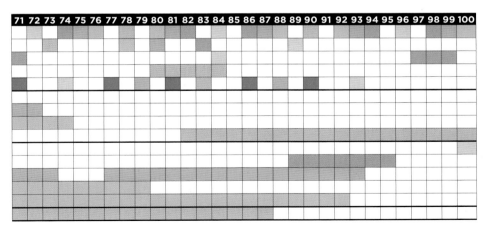

Jupiter

Keywords

Protection, Abundance, Faith, Fortune,
Generosity, Growth, Success, Wealth, Wisdom,
Excess, Extravagance, Opulence, Philosophy,
Belief System, Exploration, Knowledge

Jupiter Archetypes

The Seeker, The Explorer, The Sage,
The Wanderer, The Philosopher, The Believer

The Astronomy of Jupiter

Jupiter is, by far, the biggest planet in the solar system. Its size is so massive that you can fit all the other planets inside Jupiter and still have leftover space! This astronomy fact is relevant to grasp, as it will help you connect with Jupiter's roots as well as its effects on your life. Jupiter's size is responsible for its legendary "regal-like" attribution, named after the Roman "king of all gods" and its Greek counterpart, Zeus.

The art of astrology has developed over thousands of years of observation. Ancient astrologers noticed that Jupiter has a connection to the concept of "protection." Those of us who have a strong Jupiter in our charts tend to have this "miraculous" help from the universe—we always seem to be in the right place at the right time!

Funny enough, science just recently caught up to the fact that Jupiter casts a protective energy over planet Earth due to its astronomical effects. If the universe is so huge, with basically an infinite number of bodies traveling in it, how are we not being constantly bombarded by them? Have you ever asked yourself that? It turns out that Jupiter's gravitational pull is so powerful (due to its size) that it attracts a lot of the planetary bodies and debris that otherwise would fall into Earth's atmosphere.

The Astrology of Jupiter

In astrology, Jupiter brings the archetype of "the Great Protector" and the "Greater Benefic." Jupiter expands everything that it touches with its "Midas touch," turning what comes near it into gold! Whenever Jupiter is activated in your chart, your life, your success, your wallet, your relationships—and even your waist—expand.

Jupiter takes twelve years to complete an orbit around the Sun, meaning that the number twelve (a sacred number in many esoteric traditions) will be key whenever studying the cycles of the planet of luck. As we will study below, this means that every twelve years, Jupiter will return to the same place it was when you were born. These years can easily become the very best of your life, when luck finds you and things seem to just work out or develop in your favor.

Jupiter's Lower Vibration

But even Jupiter—yes, even the king of all planets—has a dark side. Whenever we are harnessing Jupiter's low vibration, we fall prey to laziness, excess, debauchery, and delusions of greatness. Jupiter's celestial job is to magnify—whether it's something good or bad—which is key to remember. The word *expansion* tends to have a positive connotation and, in many cases, Jupiter brings positive expansion and personal growth. However, Jupiter can also magnify a bad thing or habit.

Here's an example: Many of us experience our second Jupiter Return (more about this below) at twenty-four years old. We're feeling free and stepping into adulthood, so instead of staying focused on learning (a Jupiter activity), we party and socialize until we drop (also a Jupiter activity). Who's guilty of that? I am! You will never (at least in this incarnation) be twenty-four again, but luckily, you will experience several more Jupiter Returns. By becoming aware of them, you can avoid Jupiter's lower vibration by truly embodying its positive archetypes.

Embodying Jupiter's Higher Vibration

When it comes to embodying Jupiter's warm vibes, the phrase "make your own luck" comes to mind. When you're having a Jupiter activation, it's not a call to just sit around and wait for money and abundance to fall from the sky. Sometimes, that will happen, just naturally. But some other times, nothing will if Jupiter is not being given anything to expand. Jupiter activations are times to have faith in your natural ability to attract what you desire, while also investing your absolute very best!

Embodying Jupiter means staring at the horizon and all its possibilities, hungry for knowledge, wisdom, and experience. It involves having faith and trusting in a higher power, as Jupiter also brings the archetype of the Philosopher and the Guru. The point of predicting your Jupiter cycles brings the opportunity to push your life forward, harnessing Jupiter's momentum.

Finding Your Jupiter Sign

In your birth chart, Jupiter rules how you grow and expand, as well as your morals and overall life philosophy. Many of the blessings you were born into or that easily come your way are under Jupiter's umbrella. This is especially true if they come from mentors, benefactors, or family lineage. Since Jupiter is connected to optimism and hope, counting your blessings activates the powers of Jupiter in your birth chart.

You most likely have Jupiter in a sign different from what you see as "your sign"—around 90 percent of us do! For example, I am a Scorpio Sun, but my Jupiter is in Virgo. If you do not know your Jupiter sign, you can find it in my free online calculator by entering your year, month, day, and exact time of birth at www.naramon.com/birth-chart-calculator. Once you find it, read how your Jupiter sign manifests for you in the section below.

Your Jupiter Sign, Explained

Jupiter in Aries

If you were born with Jupiter in Aries, you love competition and courageously chase your desires. You are the epitome of a trailblazer, attracting abundance by taking the lead and often rushing into things without thinking. Luckily, Jupiter's protective vibes are (mostly) with you when you embrace a true sense of adventure, inspiring others to also embrace life with gusto and take big risks along the way. Eat the world during your Jupiter Returns, but strive to be more careful during your Jupiter Opposition years.

Jupiter in Taurus

Having Jupiter in Taurus means you own an innate sense of the value of things, which has most likely translated into a good or at least stable financial situation. You love all the good things in life and attract abundance when you share them with others. Your Returns could be very profitable years, bringing great times for business launches. Watch your appetite—for everything: food, drink, and more money—during Jupiter Opposition years, however.

Jupiter in Gemini

This planet-sign combination makes your mind and overall thought process a superpower! You are quick-witted, versatile, and highly intellectual and can move in many different social circles, as seeing many different points of view gives you perspective. A career in the written, spoken, or disseminating word might be your calling. Your Jupiter Returns probably bring extremely busy years, and your Jupiter Oppositions might definitely bring times to consider keeping some of your opinions to yourself to avoid ruffling any feathers.

Jupiter in Cancer

In astrological theory, Jupiter's absolute favorite sign to be in is Cancer. Astrologers call this an "exalted Jupiter," meaning that this planet is a force of nature in your chart. Because Cancer is the sign of family and ancestry, you have this big mama bear type of energy, and people flock to you for help, as you are a giver and a lover. More likely than not, your Jupiter activations are glorious, always growing your family, friend tribe, and community.

Jupiter in Leo

When you enter a room, all eyes are on you! Regal, magnetic, and joyous, you inspire confidence in others by bringing that warmth that characterizes you. In fact, it's your generosity what keeps bringing more riches back to you, as well as more reasons to be grateful for. Your Jupiter Returns are full of light, fame, and popularity. However, being too egotistical during your Jupiter Oppositions could either win you a couple of jealous enemies—or, at its worst, be your downfall.

Jupiter in Virgo

With this planet-sign combination, you have an important mission to fulfill in this incarnation, which involves helping, healing, or organizing others. You have incomparable attention to detail and are more likely hyperaware of your mistakes and the errors of others. You suffer from analysis paralysis due to your desire for perfection, which luckily, calms down during your Jupiter Returns. Your Jupiter Oppositions, however, are times to ground and not overextend yourself with work and deadlines.

Jupiter in Libra

Having Jupiter in Libra is like having a master's degree in public relations. How to connect, work with, and deal with people is your superpower. You have a strong sense of morals, justice, mediation, and negotiation and a keen eye for art, design, and beauty. Your Jupiter Returns are key when it comes to getting your name in high places, most likely introducing you to people who will play a key role in your life. During your Jupiter Returns, avoid overextending yourself just for the sake of pleasing others.

Jupiter in Scorpio

This planet-sign combination makes you intense but incredibly powerful. You have a laser-like ability to see the unseen and can easily get to the bottom of any puzzling situation. Psychology, research, and mysticism are your prosperous avenues for career or personal growth. While intense, your Jupiter Returns can be incredibly illuminating, full of wonderful realizations about your place in the world. During your Jupiter Oppositions, be careful not to become obsessed with something or someone.

Jupiter in Sagittarius

Lucky you—Sagittarius is one of the most positive signs for Jupiter, as the gas giant naturally rules this sign. From an early age, you probably noticed that "being in the right place at the right time" just happens to you. Worldly, adventurous, and knowledgeable, you have a tribe that follows your fun vibe. Your Jupiter Return years are most likely incredibly expansive for many areas of your life. But your Jupiter Opposition years can bring regret if you end up over-promising, over-doing, or over-spending.

Jupiter in Capricorn

If you were born with Jupiter in Capricorn, you are one industrious human! Your career as well as achieving a position of status are your priority. But at a deeper level, you are keen on building a strong foundation and leaving your mark on the world. Your Jupiter Returns bring you professional success. But because Capricorn is the opposite sign of Cancer (Jupiter's favorite sign to be in), you might have to work a little bit harder to stay optimistic in life, especially during your Jupiter Returns.

Jupiter in Aquarius

You are an innovator with a genius mind! Having Jupiter in Aquarius means you grow and expand when you allow yourself to think and do things outside of the norm. In more ways than one, you are coded to break the rules and help society imagine a better future. Your Jupiter Returns are exhilarating, but your Jupiter Oppositions can feel more intense due to the possibility of needing to choose between two paths. When in doubt, choose the most liberating option!

Jupiter Waning Square
(1, 21, 33, 45, 57, 69, 81 years old)
♃ □ ♃

Jupiter Waning Sextile
(10, 22, 34, 46, 59, 70, 82 years old)
♃ ⚹ ♃

Jupiter Waning Trine
(8, 20, 32, 44, 56, 68, 80 years old)
♃ △ ♃

Jupiter Return
(12, 24, 36, 48, 60, 72, 84 years old)
♃ ☌ ♃

Jupiter Opposition
(6, 18, 30, 42, 54, 66, 78 years old)
♃ ☍ ♃

Jupiter Waxing Sextile
(2, 14, 26, 38, 50, 62, 74 years old)
♃ ⚹ ♃

Jupiter Waxing Square
(3, 15, 27, 39, 51, 63, 75 years old)
♃ □ ♃

Jupiter Waxing Trine
(4, 16, 28, 40, 52, 64, 76 years old)
♃ △ ♃

Jupiter in Pisces

If your Jupiter is in Pisces, congratulations! From an early age, you may have noticed having some sort of "guardian angel" watching over you. This is because Jupiter naturally rules Pisces, meaning that it feels at home and can work its magic. Your Jupiter Returns years are most likely absolute magic! However, guard against excess and falling into the trap of thinking that "the universe will always provide"—especially during your Jupiter Oppositions.

YOUR JUPITER CYCLE
12 Years

Note: Your Jupiter probably won't be in this position within your chart. What this illustration seeks to convey is how your Jupiter cycle works. However, it does not include retrogrades, as each retrograde of Jupiter is unique, bringing a different flavor each time.

At left are the most important Jupiter cycles that everyone experiences. Since Jupiter changes signs every twelve months, the Jupiter cycle is relatively fast compared to the cycles of other planets such as Pluto, Uranus, and Neptune. The Jupiter Return is the most eventful within your entire Jupiter cycle, as Jupiter Returns bring years that tend to be "for the books," when Jupiter's powers push us forward to expand and explore life's biggest miracles and possibilities.

To get even more specific dates regarding your current (or next) Jupiter activations, head to this page: www.naramon.com/written-in-your-stars. Then match the results with the text below.

Strategies for Harnessing Jupiter Returns
Ages: 12, 24, 36, 48, 60, 72, 84

Every twelve years, Jupiter returns to the same position it was when you were born, meaning you experience your Jupiter Return at 12, 24, 36, 48, 60, 72, 84, and 96. Each Jupiter Return kicks off a new cycle of growth that will develop over the next twelve years. This is a time to rethink and reevaluate your relationship to your Jupiter sign. Here are some tips:

1. Embody the highest vibration of Jupiter: Seek, learn, explore, and connect. Keep your expectations low and your spirits high by focusing on searching for life's true meaning.

2. Take a big-picture approach: What do you see when taking stock of your life? If there is something you do not like, this might be a good time to change it, while you have the celestial wind at your back.

3. Put into the world the same you would like to receive: The universal "law of response" is incredibly active for you now, and you're most likely going to get more out of your Jupiter Return if you're actively giving back the same energy and attention.

4. Review your belief system: Since Jupiter rules morals, this is the ideal time to ask yourself if the way you see the world around you needs an update. If some of your views have become extreme, this is a call to bring yourself back to reality.

5. Stay optimistic and grateful: This is a fantastic time to write a list of everything life has given you, starting with the people who have helped you soar and have been there for you in life's toughest moments.

Strategies for Harnessing Your Jupiter Sextiles
Ages: 2, 10, 14, 22, 26, 34, 38, 46, 50, 59, 62, 70, 74, 82
If you're experiencing your Jupiter sextile, you are either beginning (waxing sextile) or wrapping up (waning sextile) a Jupiter cycle. Either way, many aspects of life seem to fall into place now, bringing a sense of optimism and flow into your life. The sextile is an aspect of opportunity, meaning that this is a time to open yourself to help from the universe and those around you. Here are some tips:

1. Acquire new wisdom: Philosophical Jupiter now allows you to learn and expand your mind by absorbing new information. This can be done by simply reading about a new subject, studying more formally, or experiencing new cultures and flavors that fascinate you.

2. Expand your business: If you work for a company or someone else, this could be a good time to ask for a raise or elevate your title. Authority figures will most likely be on your side, noticing your contributions. If you run your own business, this would be a good time to invest in it, as transactions and negotiations are more likely to go smoothly.

3.   Focus on what pleases you: Go ahead and fill up your cup now, while the energy is perfect for it. If you like music, listen to more of it. If you enjoy travel, visit a new place. If you're a social being, you might meet your new besties now!

Strategies for Navigating Your Jupiter Squares
Ages: 3, 9, 15, 21, 27, 33, 39, 45, 51, 57, 63, 69, 75, 81
Out of all the planetary squares, the Jupiter Square is the least noticeable due to Jupiter's positive influence. However, it can carry an energy of excess in many aspects of our lives. If you commit too much of your time, energy, and money, you could regret it later on, leaving others high and dry. Here are some tips:

1.   Watch your spending: Without noticing, you could be spending more than usual, so these years require us to have a budget and stick to it. Investments should also be handled with care now, as you could be overestimating your resources.
2.   Do not overdo it: Unfounded confidence can be an effect of the Jupiter Square, making us feel invincible. Before saying "yes," make your time or money calculations.
3.   Embrace an attitude of careful optimism: While it might sound strange, keeping your positive thinking in check is the secret to managing Jupiter's tendency toward exaggeration. Editing your "yeses" now can be your success strategy, as it opens the door to new possibilities without getting you in too much trouble.

Strategies for Harnessing Your Jupiter Trines
Ages: 4, 8, 16, 20, 28, 32, 40, 44, 52, 56, 64, 68, 76, 80
Your Jupiter Trines bring years of flow, when you're feeling optimistic about many aspects of your life. Enjoying life is easy now, but if you take the initiative to step out of your bubble to take an objective look at your life and goals, you can gain a different perspective. Here are some tips:

1.   Make plans: This is a great time to sit down and inspect your life from a big-picture perspective. Ask yourself: What's on my bucket list? Then draw a plan to achieve it. You might not need that experience now but can prepare for it while you're feeling at ease with your life.

2.   Travel and explore: This is a wonderful time to set sail on a journey, sacred pilgrimage, or spiritual exploration. At its best, it is bound to bring tremendous personal growth. At its least, you should enjoy yourself.

3.   Expand your intellectual horizons: Your mind is hungry for more now, bringing an opportunity to learn spirituality, philosophy, and languages.

4.   Take advantage of opportunities: Remember that planetary activations also come in the form of people. A mentor, teacher, or seeker could now come into your orbit to help you manifest a dream or desire.

Strategies for Navigating Your Jupiter Oppositions
Ages: 6, 18, 30, 42, 54, 66, 78

Every twelve years, Jupiter will sit exactly across from the place it was when you were born, at ages 18, 30, 42, 54, 66, 78, and 90. The "Jupiter Opposition" is not necessarily difficult, but it is mildly challenging in the sense that it makes us hungry for expansion, sometimes making us feel overly confident. During these years, the mantra "everything will work itself out" could actually backfire. Here are some tips:

1.   Avoid the lowest vibration of Jupiter: If lately you've been enjoying life's pleasures a little too much, the Jupiter Opposition could magnify that! Strive for moderation now when it comes to partying, eating, and spending.

2.   Keep an eye on your career workload: Many of your projects might come to a head or reach climax around this time, which could cause a lack of attention or, later on, exhaustion. If necessary, delay some of your commitments.

3.   Manage excess energy wisely: Restlessness could be an effect of the Jupiter Opposition, especially if you have Jupiter in a fire sign (Aries, Leo, and Sagittarius). Strenuous exercise might help ground you now.

4.   Watch your ego: If the Jupiter Opposition arrives at a good time in your life, Jupiter's feel-good vibes could come off as arrogant. This is especially true with mentors and authority figures, who, in the end, would end up winning the argument or battle.

A JUPITER CYCLE STORY

Almost everyone I know has a positive Jupiter story, but the one I'm sharing with you has a triple dose of this planet's energy! My colleague Tanaaz Chubb, an astrologer, author, and the creator of the popular website Forever Conscious, met her partner Brian in the spring of 2012, during her second Jupiter Return.

As they developed their friendship, Tanaaz was impressed with Brian's infectious optimism and ability to materialize anything he set his mind to. Being born with a very strong Jupiter, Brian started his own business at only sixteen years old and has an ability to create an idea, build it, and make it successful—over and over again. Tanaaz admired not only his career success but his ability to create a vision for his life as a whole.

In true Jupiterian form, Brian's hunger and excitement drove him to jump from one project to the next, turning everything he touched into gold—the famous Jupiter Midas touch. Brian inspired Tanaaz to dream big and forge her own path; his influence expanded her view and opened her eyes to the world of entrepreneurship. Six years later, during her Jupiter Opposition in the fall of 2018, Brian and Tanaaz tied the knot and quite recently welcomed a child.

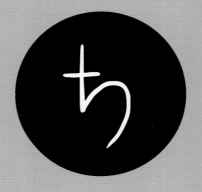

Saturn

Keywords
Mastery, Effort, Discipline, Responsibility,
Structure, Duty, Vocation, Authority, Reliability,
Karma, Contraction, Reality, Negative
Conscience, Dryness, Coldness, Boundaries

Saturn Archetypes
The Master, The Auditor, The Teacher,
The Crone, The Ruler, The Boss

The Astronomy of Saturn

Now that you've read about Jupiter, it will help you see Saturn as Jupiter's antithesis. However, to fully grasp the immense influence that the ringed planet has over our lives, it's crucial to understand its place in the solar system. When you look up to the sky, Saturn is the last visible planet to the naked eye. To ancient astrologers, who did not have telescopes, Saturn was "the end of the solar system," until 1781. And up to a hundred years later (until about the 1880s), astrology was practiced with this belief in mind. This astronomical and historical fact feeds Saturn's significance, relating it with the concepts of boundaries and limits.

Named after the Roman god of agriculture and wealth, and equated to the Greek god Cronus, Saturn was at one point exiled from Olympus by his own son, Jupiter. In mythology, Saturn is the tough father figure as well as the planetary ruler of the concept of time.

When I think about "boundaries," "exile," and other Saturn keywords like "karma," I feel a chill. Saturn's influence on us feels exactly like that, dry and chilly, which brings us to its legendary, movie-featured rings, which are unique and made of pure ice.

The Astrology of Saturn

In astrology, Saturn lives up to its tough demeanor as the archetype that sets limits, regulations, and rules. If Jupiter is the "cosmic expander," Saturn "contracts"—reducing everything that it touches to its necessary minimum. Whenever Saturn is activated in your chart, you get a reality check and are not just called—more like, pushed—to step up to the plate.

Saturn takes twenty-nine years to complete an orbit around the Sun, which is the reason why everyone alive on this planet experiences the infamous "Saturn Return" at that exact age. If you divide 29 by 4, you roughly get the number 7, so every seven years, transiting Saturn will form a hard aspect (an alignment of tension) with Saturn in your birth chart. Have you ever heard of the seven-year itch? That's literally a Saturn activation, when relationships, jobs, and all kinds of things get "tested" after being alive or active for seven years.

Saturn's Lower Vibration

Yes—life gets *real* during Saturn activations, calling on you to remove anything or anyone that is distracting you from "getting things done" or "taking care of business." We suffer Saturn's lower vibration when we ignore our responsibilities and even try to dodge the consequences of our acts. Due to Saturn's icy and cold influence, some fall into deep depression and self-alienation during these times. But at a deeper level, we are being left alone with our thoughts and responsibilities so we can figure them out.

In my counseling work, I have noticed that once an individual becomes aware of "the Saturn test" they are experiencing, they psychologically become stronger once being reassured of what they are up against. The usual question is: "How long will this last?" and make a mental note to try their absolute best until the activation ends. Once it's over, they look back feeling proud of what they accomplished.

Embodying Saturn's Higher Vibration

Saturn has a bad reputation in astrology, to the point of being feared and demonized. But, could you imagine how life would be without any reality checks? Would you enjoy the ups without the downs? During my counseling, I often describe Saturn as that grumpy old man knocking at your door ready to perform an audit of your entire life. And it is up to you to open the door and accept the invitation. Embodying the highest vibration of Saturn is ensuring you are putting your best foot forward and investing your time and energy in what is required of you at the time.

In your life, Saturn represents anything or anyone that has authority over you: your boss, the government, your parents, and even your own sense of duty and responsibility. Very often, Saturn activations are opportunities for leveling up in life, which is why many of us get married, become parents, or set new career roles around our Saturn Return, at twenty-nine or thirty years old. Saturn activations are so important that they can change our place—and status—in the world.

Finding Your Saturn Sign

In your birth chart, Saturn rules your sense of responsibility, your vocation, and how you deal with the serious areas of life. Think of Saturn as the planet that relates to the literal foundations of your home and even the bones in your body. Since Saturn rules authority figures, the zodiac sign that Saturn occupies in your chart speaks of how you were raised, the foundations of your upbringing, and how you limit yourself due to fear.

If you don't, you're in for a major discovery concerning your relationship with authority. Find your Saturn sign by entering your birth data here: www.naramon.com/birth-chart-calculator. Once you find it, read how Saturn manifests in your life below.

Your Saturn Sign, Explained

Saturn in Aries
If you were born with Saturn in Aries, you may struggle to assert yourself or showcase your leadership skills. This may have something to do with a fear of failure or not wanting to come off as egotistical. Gaining confidence in your abilities is one of your life's lessons, as is learning to take risks. Since Saturn rules time, it's crucial that, when goal-setting, you take the long view and stick to your commitments rather than expecting instant gratification.

Saturn in Taurus
Having Saturn in Taurus makes the tangible world of money, resources, and material possessions one of your life's learnings. While your focus might be to create wealth and comfort—it might also be quite difficult for you to enjoy the fruits of your labor. Learning to truly connect with your body, your five senses, and the overall concept of pleasure is your gateway to your self-growth and maybe even attracting the right romantic partner to your doorstep.

Saturn in Gemini
Being born with Saturn in Gemini involves a fear of expression, which most likely comes from an inability to speak up at an early age. While Gemini normally brings a fun energy to the table, there could be an aversion toward lighthearted conversations and behaviors. Learning to prioritize projects is a must, as it also is to communicate (write, speak, teach, and learn) with eloquence and freedom. Throat chakra meditations and clearings are recommended as a way to remove fear around self-expression.

Saturn in Cancer
Since Cancer is the sign of nurturance, having Saturn here creates a deep fear of showing vulnerability. Relating to family (especially the mother)

dynamics, this placement can create an excessive amount of responsibilities, leading to poor boundary setting. While it might be terrifying to do so, learning to open up emotionally, show vulnerability, and seek true intimacy is the way to rise above. Working with the Moon (by cycle and zodiac sign) is the gateway to living in a deeper state of flow.

Saturn in Leo

If you were born with Saturn in Leo, it might take a lot of work for you to take center stage. You have creative talents but might feel an aversion to showcasing them. Perhaps one of your parents used to take up a lot of space, which resulted in you developing a fear of behaving selfishly in front of others. One of your biggest life learnings is to express your fun and playful nature, perhaps by exploring a creative or performative career or hobby.

Saturn in Virgo

Having Saturn in Virgo means you are a perfectionist, but it can often function to your own detriment. You will know Saturn is active when instead of assisting in the process of creation, you end up in analysis paralysis. You grow and evolve when you accept your mistakes (and other people's mistakes), realizing that life doesn't need to be taken so seriously. Striving to have a manageable workload is also key to avoiding burnout, as overworking yourself could have a negative impact on your health.

Saturn in Libra

Libra is Saturn's absolute favorite sign to be in, giving you a strong sense of fairness and justice. Although you struggle with decision-making, once you commit to something or someone, you're in it for the long haul. For this reason, people (including authority figures), trust you will handle even the toughest situations with ease and grace. While you're a master in the art of relating, you might have to overcome your fear of conflict, which might involve shedding any people-pleasing tendencies.

Saturn in Scorpio

Strong and resilient, you must be a force of nature if you have this planet-sign combination! However, how easy is it for you to trust and truly be vulnerable? Learning to open up and overcome past pains and grudges is fundamental to having healthy relationships. Because, in the end, to experience deep intimacy is what your soul truly craves. Embracing change might be another area of personal growth, especially when it comes to removing yourself from less-than-desirable situations.

Saturn in Sagittarius

Sagittarius is the most optimistic sign of the zodiac, so if you have task-master Saturn here, you might have to work a little harder to find silver linings. Risk-taking is also not your favorite—but the more you learn to trust your impulses, the easier it will be to understand that life doesn't always have to make sense or be logical. Your means for personal growth are travel, learning, and physical and mental exploration. A philosophical sage shall you become as you age.

Saturn in Capricorn

Since Capricorn is one of the most comfortable signs for stern Saturn, you have a strong sense of duty and unshakable diligence. You know what you want and will not rest until you achieve it. But with such an approach, you risk behaving too rigidly, which can take the fun out of life at times. Learning to relax your high standards makes life easier for yourself and those around you, who may otherwise perceive you as cold or overly bossy.

Saturn in Aquarius

You might have felt like an outcast from an early age, because, in more ways than one, you're so different from the herd. One of your life's missions is to push society forward, but with such a big job also comes a great amount of resistance. Finding ways to add your own experimental and futuristic twists to traditional methods is part of your journey as is embracing a life and personality full of fascinating contradictions.

Saturn in Pisces

If you have Saturn in Pisces, the concept of personal boundaries might be your least favorite. But without it, you will notice life—and especially relationships—getting confusing and even messy. A highly creative being, you need to dance to the rhythm of your own drum, especially when it comes to your vocation. This deep need for freedom, however, should never be confused with escapism, as staying consistent when it comes to responsibilities is crucial to your overall success and building the life of your dreams.

YOUR SATURN CYCLE
29.5 Years
Note: Your Saturn probably won't be in this position within your chart. What this illustration seeks to convey is how your Saturn cycle works. However, it does not include retrogrades, as each retrograde of Saturn is unique, bringing a different flavor each time.

At right are the most important Saturn activations that everyone experiences. While Saturn Squares and Saturn Oppositions are very noticeable, the Saturn Return years are much more intense due to the conjunction (Saturn returning to its original point in your birth chart) being the most potent aspect in astrology.

During Saturn Sextile and Saturn Trine years, you get access to Saturn's most positive or "easiest" manifestation. During these years, you get to make headway on your goals.

To get even more specific dates regarding your Saturn activations, head to this page: www.naramon.com/written-in-your-stars. Then match the results with the text below.

Strategies for Navigating Your Saturn Returns
Ages: 29, 59, 89
Your Saturn Returns are incredibly decisive and major turning points in your life. This twenty-nine-year cycle is about the maturation of the self, making you aware of who you can become over the passage of time.

During all Saturn activations, it's crucial to embrace a "graceful aging" mentality. As the ruler of time, Saturn makes us aware that we are "getting older." If a Saturn activation is psychologically affecting you, getting an Akashic Records or Past Life Regression Reading can help you get a big-picture view of your soul's journey beyond this incarnation. Here are some tips:

1. Embody the highest vibration of Saturn: Put on your auditor hat and get to work! Treat your life as your inner garden, pruning away what is already dying so you can focus on the new story that now develops.
2. "Fear" is Saturn's number-one keyword and can function as your enemy now, to the point of paralyzing the actions that are being required of you. Whenever you feel frozen during this process, examine whether your fears about the future are unfounded (they most likely are!).

**Saturn
Waning Square**
(21, 51, 80 years old)

♄ □ ♄

**Saturn
Waning Sextile**
(24, 53, 83
years old)

♄ ⚹ ♄

**Saturn
Waning Trine**
(19, 49, 78
years old)

♄ △ ♄

**Saturn
Return**
(29, 59, 89
years old)

♄ ☌ ♄

**Saturn
Opposition**
(14, 44, 73
years old)

♄ ☌ ♄

**Saturn
Waxing Sextile**
(4, 35, 64
years old)

♄ ⚹ ♄

**Saturn
Waxing Square**
(7, 37, 66 years old)

♄ □ ♄

**Saturn
Waxing Trine**
(10, 40, 68
years old)

♄ △ ♄

3.   Is your need for isolation constructive or detrimental? Not all
     Saturn Return stories are tough. Those who have been "doing the
     work of building the life of their dreams" in previous years get a
     huge life upgrade during Saturn Returns. They become parents,
     bosses, or experience career success. If you need to isolate yourself
     to write a book or care for a baby or parent, your need for isolation
     is constructive. If you isolate yourself due to fear of the external
     world, your isolation is detrimental and could last a really long time
     if you're not careful about overcoming it.

Strategies for Harnessing Your Saturn Sextiles
Ages: 4, 24, 35, 53, 64, 83

If you are experiencing a Saturn-Saturn sextile, you are either at the very
beginning (waxing) or at the very end (waning) of your current Saturn
cycle. In both scenarios, things are moving forward for you concerning
the achievement of your goals. Since Saturn rules career goals and the
foundations of your life, you are most likely feeling a sense of balance
with the direction of your life. Here are some tips:

1.   Ages 35 and 65: You are beginning to get an idea of what your long-
     term plans look like, which will develop over the next twenty-six
     years. Sitting down to write a practical to-do list would now be
     appropriate.
2.   Ages 35 and 65: This is a great time to sit down to figure out what
     your new personal "life method" is when it comes to living a
     successful life.
3.   Ages 24, 53, 83: You are starting to get close to wrapping up a
     major Saturn cycle in your life in about four to five years, once your
     Saturn Return arrives. How can you get ahead and begin working
     toward that major rite of passage? Doing that work now can save
     you time and headaches down the road.
4.   Ages 24, 53, 83: This is a great time to start noticing how your old "life
     method" is beginning to change, slowly beginning to become obsolete,
     which you will fully notice going away during your Saturn Return.

5.   Collaborate with others: Those around you (especially authority figures) can see what you contribute, making this a wonderful time to focus on building something together.

6.   Work with a coach: Since Saturn rules authority, you can truly benefit from working with a specialist, regardless of the goal you're trying to master.

Strategies for Navigating Your Saturn Squares
Ages: 7, 21, 37, 51, 66, 80

In astrology, the square aspect brings tension and crisis between two clashing energies, so the truth is that these are trying, critical times in your life. Your mood is serious as you begin to question both past actions and the direction of your life. This is a test of your character and an opportunity to show yourself what you're made of. Here are some tips:

1.   Take the "long view": Something you began seven or even fourteen years ago (a relationship, a job, or a project) will be tested now. Ask yourself if what is being tested now can truly thrive over the next seven years, and make the appropriate changes.

2.   Draw strength during this test of your character: This is a time when obstacles, delays, and differences of opinion—especially at work— can feel weakening. Showcasing mastery over your craft is required now to overcome insecurities.

3.   Embrace endings: Relationships of all kinds get put under the microscope now, asking you to take a hard cold look at which ones you need to let go.

4.   Accept and master weaknesses: Saturn, the ultimate cosmic auditor, will show you what you are doing wrong—not to make you feel bad but to help you get your life in order. Use this time to notice flaws so you can find a way to better your life.

Strategies for Harnessing Your Saturn Trines
Ages: 10, 19, 40, 49, 68, 78
Your Saturn Trines are the most positive of all Saturn activations. This is when life, more likely than not, develops smoothly and easily, especially concerning your professional ambitions. Here are some tips:

1. Appreciate previous successes: You might receive praise for a job well done, and you should ride that wave while you can. This is evidence of your innate gifts and resilience.
2. Enjoy inner and outer stability: Your relationships are bound to feel good now since they mirror the happiness you feel inside. These years are times when you can allow yourself to deepen your connections, as you're clear of the give and take and both parties are investing the same amount of effort.
3. Reinforce your foundations: At its best, this is a preventive type of energy that can help you ensure that the bases of your life are indeed working well. By doing this, you do the preparation work before either your Saturn Opposition or Saturn Square.
4. Foster deeper professional relationships: Your bosses like you now, paving the way for more fulfilling interactions. If you are the boss, this is a great time to become closer with those who report to you.

Strategies for Navigating Your Saturn Oppositions

Ages: 14, 44, 73

Your Saturn Oppositions are times of major culminations in your life, when you reap the rewards of the efforts you have invested in the past fourteen years. Of course, there are two ways in which this activation could go. If you've worked toward building the life of your dreams, this activation could mean landing your dream job or a situation you've worked hard to achieve. In the case that you have not, Saturn will do you a favor by showing you *what* went wrong and *how* you begin turning your life around. Here are some tips:

1. Go down memory lane: What have you neglected over the past seven or fourteen years? If it is your body, your family, or your finances, this is the time to get things right by bringing attention to that area of your life. If, on the contrary, you've been balancing your life, the effects of this opposition will be lesser felt. In fact, Saturn Oppositions could be very productive times. You are reaping the consequences of your actions—whether they are good or bad.

2. Seek balance by working with your Saturn's sign polarity: In astrology, polarities or "sister signs" are our go-to when working with oppositions. For example, someone with Saturn in Capricorn would normally be very ambitious and career-oriented. During a Saturn Opposition, which would happen during the time Saturn is traveling in Cancer, this individual will most likely need to take time away from work (or at least work less) to divert their energy toward taking care of family affairs.

3. Ask yourself: What is standing between me and my dream life? Once you get to the bottom of your response, consider leaving it behind while Saturn's influence supports you in performing an energetic cleansing.

4. Age 44: Depending on when you experience your other midlife crisis activations (either your Uranus Opposition or Neptune Square), this can feel like a confusing time. Resolve to realize that from the chaos you might be experiencing there is an opportunity for creating something new.

MY MOM'S SATURN SQUARE STORY—
HOW I CAME INTO THIS WORLD!

My mother, Paty, has an interesting Saturn story. As someone whose birth chart is very Saturn-heavy (she has her Sun, Moon, Mercury, Venus, Rising Sign, and Saturn all in Sagittarius!), it was written in her stars to mature faster than most people.

As a kid and teenager, Paty was an excellent student who spent most of her time reading and studying. By age twenty, she had already stayed faithful to her Sagittarian nature (this is the sign ruling knowledge and foreign culture) and already knew how to speak and write English and French quite well, besides her native Spanish.

In December 1978, while shopping for clothes for an upcoming event, she ran into a tall, handsome, olive-skinned, green-eyed gentleman named Jorge Alberto, who was originally from Honduras. She fell in love with him, to the point of introducing him to her friends and family that same month (Sagittarians are unapologetically fast!).

Paty and Jorge Alberto continued their whirlwind romance, and by the time Valentine's Day 1979 was over, they were pregnant (with me) and just a few months later, decided to marry. Nine months later, I was born on November 11, exactly when Paty's Saturn Waning Square (twenty-one years old) was beginning to take shape. The following year and a half was incredibly busy and life-changing for her. Besides now being married and becoming a mother, Paty was finishing college during the day while working as a receptionist at night.

This is not only a classic Saturn story of change in status and heightened responsibility but also illustrates the very specific relationship a person—in this case, Paty—can have with one planet. For her, Saturn (responsibility, work, and self-mastery) in Sagittarius (spontaneous, foreign, and intellectual) was and continues to be a life staple.

Now, at sixty-six years old, Paty is living this planet-sign combination differently. For more than thirty years, she has owned a restaurant on one of the most beautiful beaches in Mexico, which is visited by locals but also by people from all over the world.

At a deeper level, Paty's birth chart always pointed at someone who was meant to grow faster than most of the people from her generation. The good news is that, to this day, she still says that giving birth to her only daughter was the best thing that has happened to her.

Chiron

Keywords
Healing, Holistic, Bridge, Spiritual Warrior,
Acceptance, Integration, Gift, Being of Service,
Shamanism, Pain, Abandonment, Resilience,
Alienation, Broken, Unlocking, Wholeness

Chiron Archetypes
The Wounded Healer, The Mentor,
The Astrologer, The Therapist,
The Cosmic Key

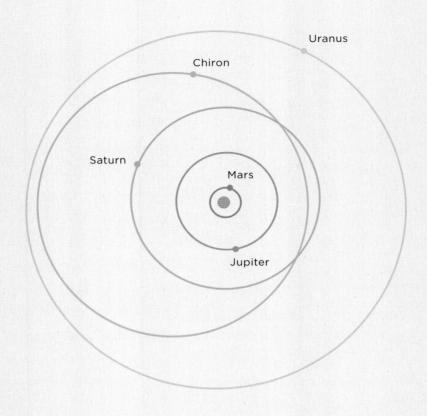

The Astronomy of Chiron

Chiron was the first member of a new class of over three hundred celestial bodies categorized as "centaurs." Traveling between the Asteroid Belt and the Kuiper Belt, centaurs are bigger than asteroids with a comet-like composition. It is this dual nature (half asteroid/half comet) that inspired astronomer Charles Kowal to name Chiron after the wise Greek mythological centaur (half human/half horse) in 1977.

This duality and dichotomy are present in everything we have so far studied about Chiron—astronomically and astrologically. Even Chiron's orbit is locked into the orbits of two other planets: Saturn and Uranus. This astronomical fact is crucial to getting to understand Chiron, as it is the planetary body that unites the last visible planet (Saturn), with the first invisible planet (Uranus). Adding to its enigma, Chiron's orbit is eccentric (shown above) and quite unstable, meaning that its effects are way more unpredictable than the effects of the actual planets.

The Astrology of Chiron

Everything you've read about the astronomy of Chiron applies to its potent astrological meaning. From immense pain and suffering to the ultimate state of wholeness, Chiron's symbolism represents the full spectrum of the spiritual journey.

In mythology, centaurs were wild beings who easily fell prey to violence and self-destructive behaviors. Unlike regular centaurs who were four-legged, Chiron had two front legs and was morally and spiritually more elevated. Although he was abandoned by his mother (sea nymph Philyra) and was physically wounded, Chiron became a healer, a wise mystic, and a shamanic initiator of many notable figures.

Known as the Wounded Healer, Chiron's position in your birth chart speaks of the deepest wound you carry in this incarnation. These wounds vary in nature, coming from childhood, societal pre-conditioning, being psychical—and in some cases, even coming from a past life. These wounds are never easy to approach—after all, Chiron was just discovered in 1977! Barbara Hand Clow, in her pioneering book *Chiron, Rainbow Bridge*, affirms, "The sighting of Chiron coincided with the late 1970s surge in channeling, divination, body/mind healing, homeopathic medicine, and multidimensional perceptual skills."

Chiron's Lower Vibration

Every one of us has Chiron in our charts—but some of us have it more pronounced than others. Living under Chiron's lower vibration means we are still living by our deepest pain. Even worse, we don't talk about it, we just can't, because it stings so deeply with us, that we prefer to pretend it is not there or that it didn't happen. Especially, when we don't talk about it, it festers deep inside, making us feel like we are the only ones who suffered this wound. When really, the human experience is about patterns that repeat, meaning that there are others who, like us, have had similar experiences. Chiron's lower vibration equals the phrase "unhealed trauma," which, as we've come to find out, gets stored in the psyche.

Here's the most interesting part about Chiron: Because astronomically, Chiron is the bridge between the visible and the invisible planets, and the invisible planets (Uranus, Neptune, and Pluto) represent one's spiritual self, when we don't heal our Chiron, we lose our connection with our higher self. That's why, to become a healer, you must heal your own wound first.

Embodying Chiron's Higher Vibration

In astrology, every planetary symbol holds a deeper meaning—and in the case of Chiron, its symbol features a key. Some astrologers (myself included) believe Chiron is the key to unlocking the entire birth chart. In other words: the wound is the key, and by unlocking it, you unearth the unique gift that you came to share with the world.

Embodying Chiron's higher vibration means seeking the deeper meaning of the wound you carry. It means turning a "what happened to me" into a "it happened for me" mentality. Often, this healing is achieved by embracing and diving deeply into natural, homeopathic, therapeutic, psychological, and esoteric practices. Although there are some painful life moments we can't change, Chiron teaches us that with self-love and self-study we can turn hurt into healing, wounds into wisdom, and pain into power.

Finding Your Chiron Sign

Since Chiron is a slow-moving body, its meaning is shared by entire generations. But due to its highly irregular orbit, Chiron doesn't spend the same amount of time in each sign. Chiron spends the most time in Aries, which is around eight years, while the shortest duration is in Libra, which is only about one-and-a-half to two years.

To find your Chiron sign, enter your exact day and time of birth in my calculator: www.naramon.com/birth-chart-calculator. Once you find it, read about how you can turn pain into healing and wounds into wisdom.

Your Chiron Sign, Explained

Chiron in Aries

If your Chiron is in Aries, your wound is about self-assertion, leadership, and identity. Perhaps you were exposed to toxic masculinity, learning from a young age that you did not want to follow those steps. Your power unlocks when you learn how to cultivate your masculine side. Once you overcome the insecurity of being unable to show yourself exactly as you are, the sky's the limit! You can become a trailblazer, unafraid of chasing the unique path that you came to build for yourself.

Chiron in Taurus

Chiron in Taurus means there is a wound you must overcome around money, pleasure, or personal values. In the end, all these topics are about overcoming deep issues of self-worth, most likely coming from loss or family dynamics when young. You attract the life of your dreams when you fully allow yourself to sink into the type of pleasure that your soul craves to experience. Creativity plays a big role in bringing you back to bliss and creating a deeper connection to your soul.

Chiron in Gemini

I have read for a lot of people with this combination and have found that they all have a wound around communication. For various reasons, people with this combination weren't comfortable speaking up, which has prevented them from speaking their truth. If you have this combination, you have a gift for teaching, writing, public speaking, or some type of information dissemination. The healing comes when you feel free to express yourself exactly as you are and help others do the same.

Chiron in Cancer

Since Cancer is the sign of family and the mother, Chiron in Cancer relates to a deep wound around nurturance. This could even extend to the entire concept of ancestral trauma, which would require a lot of deep spiritual work that would release you from karmic ties within your past lives. Parenting yourself the way you were not becomes the most radical act of self-love and self-acceptance as it also creates the home and family life you so much crave.

Chiron in Leo

Ruled by the Sun, Leo is the sign of self-expression, so having Chiron in this sign brings a wound around the fear of being seen. This could be especially true if you were born at night. Perhaps your parents were too strict or critical, impeding your self-expression. Having a creative hobby—or even better, a creative career—is your way to trust your immense imagination. Creating just to create without needing anyone's approval or permission is your gateway to freedom and success.

Chiron in Virgo

As the sign of wellness, Virgo is the healer of the zodiac and, therefore, one of the most powerful signs for Chiron. You might have run into some sensitivities from a young age, taking you on a healing path to better and deepen your mind/body/spirit connection. Eventually, you might even decide to make the jump from holistic living to a health-focused career. You are a natural-born healer, and being of service is the way to reach your full potential.

Chiron in Libra

Very few people have Chiron in Libra, but those who do have a wound around relationships. You must learn to relate from a place of uniqueness and individuality, avoiding comparing yourself to others just for the sake of belonging. Becoming addicted to company or constantly beginning and ending relationships gets cured by finding strength in embracing the solo journey. Alternatively, a career in therapy or people's management is another way to take the "people's person" focus off your personal life.

Chiron in Scorpio

Scorpio is the sign of sexuality, intimacy, and control or power dynamics within relationships—so if you are one of the few that have this combination, you find it hard to truly trust. This combination is the epitome of the "shama's journey," inspiring deep work with psychotherapy, plant medicine, Kundalini awakening, or esoteric practices. Truly learning that the power of your sexuality is not attached to anything or anyone is when you take your power back. Once healed, you become an agent of positive change for others, too.

Chiron in Sagittarius

If you have Chiron in Sagittarius, you came into this incarnation with a deep wound around faith and trust in a higher power. You are a wise soul who lost your way (and deep knowledge) along the way. This combination is about remembering your innate gifts by diving into philosophy, metaphysics, physics, and even unearthing the truth about life and the mysteries of the universe. Your power returns when you revive your connection with the magic that comes from ancient knowledge.

Chiron in Capricorn

Having Chiron in Capricorn means you probably had a very strict parent (most likely father), which resulted in a wound around pressure to succeed and achieve. Alternatively, an absent parent could have also undermined your confidence in achieving your most cherished goals. Healing family dynamics and any type of lack mentality is crucial for your growth, as you came to this incarnation to succeed, shine, and build something meaningful that will last the test of time.

Chiron in Aquarius

Aquarius is the outcast of the zodiac, so having Chiron in this sign means there has always been a part of you that feels left out, "out of this world," or disconnected from the collective. But it's in this uniqueness and weirdness where your brilliance resides! Giving birth to new and groundbreaking ideas is our gift to the world, but it can only be done when you manage to ground yourself through deep meditative states and energetic chakra healing and alignment.

Chiron in Pisces

Chiron in Pisces can bring a deep wound around loss, faith, or spirituality. You are an incredibly sensitive soul who might struggle with boundaries—and, therefore, can be easily hurt by others if not careful. Protecting your energy with crystals and visualization is key as is developing limits within your relationships. Your true gift comes when you learn to trust your intuition, developing your psychic and creative abilities so you can put them in service to humanity.

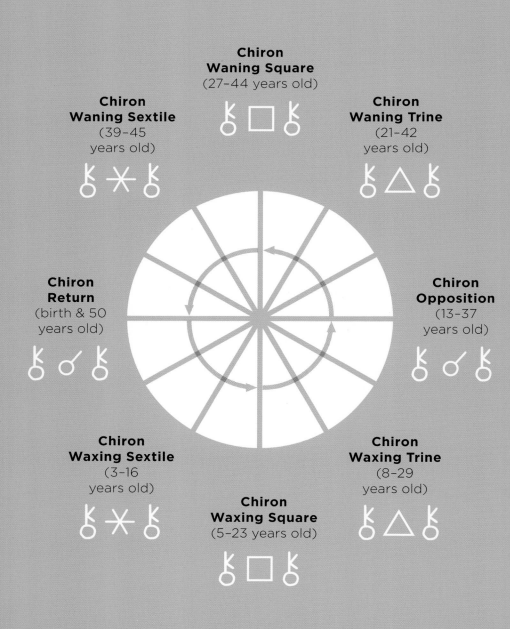

Chiron Waning Square
(27–44 years old)

Chiron Waning Sextile
(39–45 years old)

Chiron Waning Trine
(21–42 years old)

Chiron Return
(birth & 50 years old)

Chiron Opposition
(13–37 years old)

Chiron Waxing Sextile
(3–16 years old)

Chiron Waxing Square
(5–23 years old)

Chiron Waxing Trine
(8–29 years old)

YOUR CHIRON CYCLE
50 Years
Note: Your Chiron probably won't be in this position within your chart. What this illustration seeks to convey is how your Chiron cycle works. However, it does not include retrogrades, as each retrograde of Chiron is unique, bringing a different flavor each time.

Chiron is not a planet and, therefore, does not behave like one. The Wounded Healer centaur's orbit is irregular (elliptical), meaning that its effects vary from generation to generation. For example, someone with Chiron in Aries will experience their first Chiron Square (waxing square) between sixteen and nineteen years old; and the activation will last for about six to nine months. A Chiron in Libra native will experience it as young as six to eight years old. However, for them, the activation will only last for about one to three months. The same happens with the Chiron Opposition as well as the second Chiron Square (waning square).

The Chiron Return, however, is very predictable, as Chiron takes between fifty and fifty-one years to perform a full loop around the zodiac. We all experience our Chiron Return around that age. When we are finished with our first Chiron Return, at around fifty-one years old, the cycle begins all over again.

To get even more specific dates regarding your current (or next) Chiron activations, head to this page: www.naramon.com/written-in-your-stars. Then match the results with the text below.

Strategies for Navigating Your Chiron Return
Ages: 50 to 51
Like the Uranus Opposition, your Chiron Return is one of the most impactful rites of passage of your life. Incredibly transformative, your Chiron Return is the last of your "midlife crisis" activations. The physical changes, which can have psychological effects in your body, are obvious, as you are entering a new decade. Yes, you are getting older—but what Chiron truly wants to know is: Are you also getting wiser? Here are some tips:

1. Resolve to abandon any unhealthy habits: After battling addictions for many years, I have seen clients making huge comebacks at their Chiron Return. This happens by replacing a bad habit with a positive one. Like, for example, replacing drinking with meditation, walks in nature, or studying.
2. Cultivate acceptance: You will notice old themes (even those you seemed to have overcome) coming back now to be reviewed. A deep sense of self-love and self-acceptance is required now so you can move forward with the next step.
3. Seek deep healing: If you haven't yet dealt with your Chiron wound, it will become very obvious now as it catches up with you. You will notice unhealed traumas coming back now. Choose your modality—Reiki, psychotherapy, shamanic healing, or eye movement desensitization and preprocessing (EMDR) therapy—and stick to it until the activation is over.
4. Embrace reinvention: Avoid thinking that at this age, you're "too old" to make a big life change. If the universe is showing you a redirection, it means you must explore it. This might include moving to a career that allows you to turn your wound into your superpower and put it in service of others.

Strategies for Harnessing Your Chiron Sextile
Ages: 3 to 16, 39 to 45

Similar to Pluto's, Chiron's activations are felt intensely, even if they involve an easy aspect, like the sextile, as everything that Chiron rules in our lives runs deep and feels very personal. Due to the wide range of ages during which we all experience our first Chiron sextile, we must look at the first and second sextile activations separately. Here are some tips:

1. Age 3 to 16: Your awareness of your first Chiron-Chiron activation will depend on how old you get to experience it. Consciously or unconsciously, you are receiving the opportunity to heal, meaning that something in your life most likely gets better now. If you happen to experience this closer to your teen years, this is a wonderful time to dive into any esoteric or holistic practices so you can discover your natural ability to heal—or even better, start unraveling your life's purpose.

2. Age 39 to 45: The second Chiron sextile prepares you for your Chiron Return (which arrives at fifty). Regardless of where your Chiron sign is, you are now in crunch time to overcome your Chiron wound. By seeking to heal yourself at the deepest level now, you set yourself up for success. Seek energetic healing via Reiki, past life regressions, sound therapy, art therapy, and spiritual and esoteric practices.

Strategies for Navigating Your Chiron Squares
Ages: 5 to 23, 27 to 44

You read it in the first chapter of this book: the square is an aspect of crisis, which is specifically true when it comes to Chiron's involvement. Both, the first (waxing) and the second (waning) square, highlight the Chiron wound—the difference is that the waxing square gives birth to it, and the waning square brings a resurgence of it. Here are some tips:

1. Develop your mystical side: Flashes of intuition, out-of-body experiences, or kundalini awakenings are possible now, and they mean you are evolving as a human being. The intuitive skills that are being born now could later turn into allies, so don't hide from them or try to suppress them. Instead, follow your spiritual bliss!
2. Navigate sexual urges: Chiron's most primal side comes out the strongest now, manifesting as intense sexual urges and spiritually driven erotic experiences. Especially with the first square, explore your sexuality in ways that are liberating but healthy.
3. Find the middle ground between belonging and alienation: You might now experience a realization concerning what sets you apart from your clan. Instead of feeling shame for being different, try figuring out how what distinguishes you from your friends, family, or society that can be reshaped into a gift.

Strategies for Harnessing Your Chiron Trine
Age: 8 to 29, 21 to 42

Out of all Chiron activations, this is the most positive one. Things line up for you to become more aware of your sore spot so you can begin resolving that you are not your wound. Especially during the first trine (eight to twenty-nine years old), this is a time of acceptance, which eventually leads to alchemizing pain into power. Here are some tips:

1. Voice your wound: Something magical happens when we're able to speak or talk about our traumas from a more detached perspective. By doing so now, you could even meet others with a similar healing path to yours.
2. Receive help: The people who come into your life now could be catalysts for you to overcome old pain or insecurities. Mythological Chiron was a wise teacher, and its influence can come now in the form of a healer, teacher, or mentor showing up to assist your healing process.
3. Welcome spiritual awakenings: Out-of-body experiences, magical dreams, or visions are possible now, and they represent spiritual awakenings. Instead of repressing them, follow the signs, as they could lead you to a closer connection with your spirit guides.
4. Learn astrology: Chiron might have been the first astrologer ever, so when you have your Chiron Trine, getting insight into your birth chart can be a major turning point in your life.

Strategies for Navigating Your Chiron Opposition
Ages: 13 to 37

In astrology, the opposition is an aspect that requires balance, meaning that to feel more complete, you might have to bring different energies, getting out of your comfort zone to find wholeness. To grow and evolve, Chiron's dual nature as both a centaur and a wise teacher must be embraced now, bridging the primal and intellectual parts of ourselves. Here are some tips:

1. Cultivate balance between body and intellect as well as the material with the immaterial: The truth is that most of us are imbalanced, which becomes extremely obvious at our Chiron Opposition. If you're too caught up in working hard and creating wealth, seek to develop your sense of spirituality. Similarly, if you spend too much time meditating and disconnected from the reality of life, this is the time to put your feet on the ground and work toward practical goals.
2. Monitor projection: Watch that you don't consciously or unconsciously attribute your feelings, values, traumas, or phobias to others. Examining the tensions that come up in your relationships now will give you insights into what you need to heal and work on.
3. Find purpose and meaning: Because Chiron relates to putting ourselves in the service of others or humanity, this is a fabulous time to step into our soul path. To find yours, dive into your Lunar North Node—by sign, astrological house, and aspect.

CHIRON CYCLES: PERSONAL STORIES

One of my clients, Maria O'Rourke, has one of the most inspiring Chiron Return stories I have witnessed. Having a brilliant mind, Maria worked for a pharmaceutical company for almost thirty years. She started as a generic researcher in biochemistry and rose in the ranks after earning a master's degree in organization leadership. She became an executive director leading a large clinical operations organization. Many would think this is a decent profession, but for Maria, this was a regression when it comes to the evolution of her soul. In her past lives, she had been a doctor, a nurse, and a pharmacist many times over—so in this lifetime, she is meant to move away from that. Her North Node in Pisces (soul path) is all about walking the spiritual path while being of service by integrating all the learnings of her past lives (Virgo).

Since she was flowing in the opposite direction of what her soul craved, Maria developed an alcohol addiction that lasted for decades. When her Chiron Return started in the summer of 2022, she momentarily quit drinking but soon relapsed. By the fall, she fully realized her lifestyle (job and addiction) was killing her—she had her last drink and began doing some deep soul searching. Maria had never believed in astrology, but when she dared to look into it, she got hooked! Her kids gifted her my book *Moon Sign: Unlock Your Inner Luminary Power*, which is how we got connected.

In the spring of 2023, Maria decided to enroll in a school of evolutionary astrology and was on her way to becoming a professional reader. A month later, she had her first psychic awakening, when her spirit guides began showing up to guide her during her meditations. By the fall of 2023, she was giving mediumship sessions to clients and had also enrolled in hypnosis healing training. When her Chiron Return was over (in February 2024), she quit her corporate job and launched her private practice as a professional astrologer, medium, and hypnotherapist. Maria's dedication to her practice is admirable and it's amazing to see her thrive after knowing what she was up against for so many years. Her story also proves that it is never too late to turn things around!

Uranus

Keywords
Liberation, Freedom, Radical Change,
Innovation, Inspiration, Intuition, Individuality,
Creativity, Electricity, Breakdown, Breakthrough,
Revolution, Chaos, Restlessness

Uranus Archetypes
The Maverick, The Inventor, The Genius,
The Eccentric, The Rebel,
The Awakener

The Astronomy of Uranus

Now that you've read about Saturn, it will help you see Uranus as the planetary influence that breaks everything Saturn builds. The correlation between astronomy, astrology, and human consciousness truly took flight starting in the late 1700s, with the discovery of Uranus. When this planet was first sighted in 1781, humans were experiencing the Industrial Revolution as well as the French and American revolutions.

Saturn becoming "the last *visible* planet" began changing our entire perspective of the solar system—and, therefore, the universe. This astronomical and societal fact gives Uranus its place in our lives as the "disruptor" and the "revolutionary" planet that arrived to break everything that, for centuries, we considered true or real. To top it off, Uranus is the only planet in the solar system that rotates differently—instead of rotating horizontally, Uranus rotates vertically, on its own belly.

Seen through the lens of mythology, Uranus sticks to its unorthodox nature. Named after the god Ouranus, the creator of sky and earth associated with lightning, Uranus also has strong connections to another god: Prometheus, the humanitarian Titan who stole the fire from the gods to gift it to humanity, along with other arts of civilization. In both myths, we find Uranus' creative power and brilliance that can only be accessed when we dare to go beyond the material.

The Astrology of Uranus

Astrologically speaking, Uranus brings in the archetype of the Awakener—it's that lightning bolt of energy that runs through your spine, bringing an aha moment and awakening your intuition. It sounds fun, and it is, but to get to that moment of epiphany and even ecstasy, there needs to be a liberation of the mind.

Astrologer Jeff Green, in his legendary book *Uranus, Freedom from the Unknown*, refers to Uranus as the planet correlating to individuation, liberation, freedom, and deconditioning: "If Saturn relates to all conditioning patterns in your life, including conditioning patterns of society, family, and expectations of people in your life, Uranus is forever trying to shatter, revolutionize, and break free from those patterns." Uranus seeks to liberate you from all the filters you naturally absorb so you can easily arrive at and express your own unique essence.

Uranus' Lower Vibration

The absolute truth is that embodying Uranus is not easy for most of us for two reasons: the fear of change and the fear of showing ourselves as we truly are. This response to Uranus has a lot to do with how the planet is positioned in each one of our birth charts, by zodiac sign, astrological house, and aspect.

Jeff Green affirms that only 30 percent of the population has this planet's energy integrated into their psyche and, therefore, behavior. This means that 70 percent of us are likely to struggle to respond to Uranus activations. Put another way: 30 percent of us seek to live life according to our own values and desires, while 70 percent of us comply with what others expect of us. Naturally, it would make sense that during Uranian activations, those in the 70 percent group will need to work harder to integrate the freedom-seeking energy of Uranus. Which group are you in?

When responding negatively to a Uranus activation, we resist change and do everything in our power (consciously or unconsciously) to maintain the status quo. Alternatively, we behave too erratically and impulsively. Uranian brilliance is trying to speak to us, but we don't listen, which leads to restlessness and a disconnection from our intuition.

Embodying Uranus' Higher Vibration

The Uranian liberation comes in the form of surprising events, sudden endings, and unexpected twists and turns. We get jolted out of complacency—and suddenly, the master plan we had created in our minds no longer applies. The role of Uranus is to show us that the plan we first envisioned was too restrictive, perhaps lacking playfulness and creativity. Going even further, perhaps it wasn't aligned with our true essence, which in this case, we would know right away due to a feeling of euphoric liberation.

Embodying the highest vibration of Uranus means going with the flow, understanding that all these changes, regardless of their nature, are happening *for us* and not against us. Of course, this also means being comfortable with the unknown and approaching life with curiosity and excitement. Since Uranus is connected to intuition, we channel its higher vibration when we open our minds to the intangible side of life. We are being given the opportunity to ideate groundbreaking, out-of-the-box ideas.

Finding Your Uranus Sign

Finding your Uranus sign is relatively easy, as Uranus is a generational planet, so there is a strong chance that most of your friends from your age have the same Uranus sign as you. To find your Uranus sign, enter your exact day and time of birth in my calculator: www.naramon.com/birth-chart-calculator. Once you find it, read how you approach uniqueness, liberation, rebellion, and freedom.

Your Uranus Sign, Explained

Uranus in Aries

If you were born with Uranus in Aries, you find it easier to embrace change than most folks. You might even jump into change too quickly at times. The epitome of a maverick, you're swift at coming up with great ideas but might need someone else's support to bring them to reality. During your Uranus activations (especially the Uranus Opposition at 42 to 44), you might experience an identity crisis, pushing you to reinvent yourself. Overall, you evolve when you embrace the ongoing process of self-discovery.

Uranus in Taurus

Since Taurus is the zodiac sign that rules a pleasurable connection to the body, you rebel against the mainstream ways of seeing and experiencing sensuality. Automatically, this means you need the freedom to create your own value system, not only concerning pleasure but also lifestyle, money, and material resources. During Uranus activations, you're bound to feel a deep need for sexual and relationship experimentation, especially during the exciting Uranus Opposition. If you haven't found liberation by then, expect your world to be truly shaken!

Uranus in Gemini

You have a fast and brilliant mind. Gemini is about communication, writing, speaking, and learning—so part of your journey is to revolutionize how the human mind processes information. You are a walking incubator of ideals but might struggle a bit to give them form due to your propensity to be easily bored. Since you're highly intellectual, your Uranus activations can be specifically restless, asking you to practice grounding. This will be especially true during your Uranus Opposition, around your early forties.

Uranus in Cancer

Cancer is the sign of the mother, home, culture, and ancestry—so you naturally rebel against traditional ways of approaching family. You prefer to create your own family dynamics outside of what is "normal," and might even need to find your "tribe" outside your bloodline to find a sense of belonging. This might be especially true as you enter your forties, when a real feeling of liberation from the past finds you. Overall, learning to navigate your emotional ups and downs is crucial.

Uranus in Leo

A tremendous source of creativity lives within you, but it often goes unchanneled due to a strong fixation on going against the rules. A force of nature, you challenge authority, but you must always strive to be a rebel with—and not without—a cause. The artistic and performative arts could be your playground and a way to boldly express your unique identity. If by your early forties, you haven't found a way to express your creative nature, expect to have a radical awakening of the soul!

Uranus in Virgo

Ruling over health, wellness, and healing, Virgo is the zodiac sign that oversees the overall mind-body-spirit connection. Part of your journey is to innovate how humans approach such an important synergy, which is crucial to feeling and becoming whole. You're insightful and can find brilliant solutions to any problem. You can develop incredible intuition as long as you don't allow your logical mind to take over. If it does, a serious disconnect can take place, which would most likely manifest during your Uranus Opposition.

Uranus in Libra

Libra is the zodiac sign that rules justice, beauty, art, and design as well as relationships. Having change-maker Uranus in this sign means you're breaking the mold in one or many of those areas. Especially when it comes to relating, you need the freedom to interact with folks from all walks of life, as this is your means to find your own sense of individuality. Without this room to explore, you risk experiencing an imminent breakup by your early forties.

Uranus in Scorpio

Scorpio is believed to be the strongest sign for Uranus, making you a deep, penetrating, and magical human. An avid self-analyzer, you're practically allergic to superficiality and have a laser-like ability to see below facades, which can make some people uncomfortable. You rebel against anything or anyone who strives to have power over you, as the end goal is to reach full psychological and emotional freedom. If you haven't achieved this by your early forties, expect to experience a radical change in your life.

Uranus in Sagittarius

Having Uranus in Sagittarius makes you an inspirational awakener, opening society's eyes to spiritual, cultural, religious, and philosophical truths. A free soul and thinker, you ask all the questions no one dares to even imagine. You go against the classic forms of absorbing information, preferring to learn (and teach) through experience. Your Uranus activations can bring mind-shattering realizations about the world and your place in it. But if handled correctly, your Uranus Opposition can be the source of brilliant idea-birthing.

Uranus in Capricorn

Capricorn is the zodiac sign that rules career, business, authority, the government, and the status quo. While you're not super loud in your rule-breaking, you do take it seriously! In the end, you can see the real damage in these systems because you've lived the consequences of your elders' decision-making. Your Uranian activations are all about peeling off the layers of parental and societal preconditioning. If handled right, your Uranus Opposition could feel like a soul-nurturing comeback to the "real you."

Uranus in Aquarius

In modern astrological theory, Uranus rules Aquarius, meaning that you have a strong relationship with this maverick, innovative planet. You know the rules really well—but it is mainly to know how to break them and get away with it! You have a brilliant mind, adept for science, technology, and all things futuristic. The strong mission of activism is part of your journey, which most likely becomes obvious during Uranus activations. A creative outlet for your hyperactive mind becomes necessary as you approach your early forties.

Uranus in Pisces

Pisces is the zodiac sign that rules spirituality, music, culture, and artistic vision. These are your means for seeking freedom and liberation, most likely taking you from one transformation to the next. Your chameleon-like nature allows you to experiment with a wide variety of styles, as your brilliance is awakened when you attune to mass consciousness. Learning to trust your intuition is key, especially during Uranus Squares. At your Uranus Opposition, seek a balance between the left and right sides of the brain.

YOUR URANUS CYCLE
84 Years

Note: Your Uranus probably won't be in this position within your chart. What this illustration seeks to convey is how your Uranus cycle works. However, it does not include retrogrades, as each retrograde of Uranus is unique, bringing a different flavor each time.

On page 92 are the most important Uranus activations that everyone experiences at specific ages, with the Uranus Opposition being the most important to pay attention to. Your Uranus activations tend to be very noticeable, as Uranus is the planet of excitement, change, surprises, and genius energy, bringing electrifying effects to your life.

To get even more specific dates regarding your current (or next) Uranus activations, head to this page: www.naramon.com/written-in-your-stars. Then match the results with the text below.

Strategies for Navigating Your Uranus Return
Age: 84

Not many of us make it to the Uranus Return—but if we do, this can be a time of spiritual awakening. By now, you've hopefully crossed off all the items on your bucket list and you are ready to chill. Now there is the realization that you could die at any moment—and isn't that the ultimate form of liberation? Here are some tips:

1. Western society demonizes death, but as we mystics know, there are two other processes called "afterlife" and "reincarnation." This would be a great time to read and learn about these processes, as they can get you closer to understanding "the eternity of the human soul."

Uranus Waning Square (63–65 years old)

Uranus Waning Sextile (69–71 years old)

Uranus Waning Trine (55–57 years old)

Uranus Return (birth & 84 years old)

Uranus Opposition (39–45 years old)

Uranus Waxing Sextile (13–15 years old)

Uranus Waxing Square (20–22 years old)

Uranus Waxing Trine (28–30 years old)

2. Adopt a creative hobby: Uranus can be a colorful planet full of excitement—and during this time it is active in your chart, it could even awaken some dormant gifts you never thought you had or cared to explore.
3. If you haven't retired by now, this is the perfect time to truly liberate yourself!

Strategies for Harnessing Your Uranus Sextiles
Ages: 13 to 15, 69 to 71

The Waxing Uranus Sextile (the first of two), happening between thirteen and fifteen years old, is a transitional rite of passage between childhood and adulthood and the astrological reason behind the rebellious adolescence. The second one (Waning Uranus Sextile), arriving at seventy years old, is more about reflecting on one's life and what we got from it. Here are some tips:

1. You're no longer a kid, so act accordingly: Whether you're fourteen or seventy, this is your biggest revelation now! If fourteen, this is exciting, so strive to become more independent. If seventy, strive to break free from the past, as the universe is paving the way for you.
2. It's okay to question everything: This is your opportunity to healthily challenge all that society has told you about life. If you handle this right, you can find a great amount of freedom.
3. Age 15: You might now begin rebelling against authority or the status quo—and if you're smart in your approach, it's easier to get away with it. By being open about how you feel, others might understand you better.
4. Age 15: Explore your sexuality in healthy ways: Many of us begin feeling sexual desires at this age, and there is nothing to be ashamed of. Begin exploring this with people who you truly trust.
5. Age 70: More likely than not, you are free to explore life without worrying about some of your former responsibilities. Sit down and ask yourself if you lived life to your own values. If the answer is no, now is the perfect time for some course-correction.
6. Age 70: Reevaluate your future goals, leaving behind what you no longer need to make room for what you truly desire of your precious time.

Strategies for Navigating Your Uranus Squares
Ages: 20 to 22, 63 to 65

Knocking at your door during major transitional years, your Uranus squares can bring a ton of rapid change to your life. Since the square is an aspect of crisis and tension, this is when you might feel the nervous energy of this planet—its lowest vibration—the most. Here are some strategies to help you navigate them:

1. Age 22: Adopt a "rebel with a cause" mentality: This is an age when we want to challenge authority—but it matters *how* you do it! If you do it correctly, you avoid getting into too much trouble. After all, this year is about exploring your sense of individuality.

2. Age 63: The effects of this Uranus square will greatly depend on how you handled your Uranus Opposition at 42. If you prioritized your own values over those of others, this year might not be as intense. If you pushed yourself to conform, then this might be a good time to catch up with your true desires. It's never too late to seek the freedom your soul craves!

3. Age 63: If you were very career-focused and decide to retire now, strive to find a true life outside of your work or career. Then this year would be about finding the "true" meaning of life.

4. Take disruptions as opportunities for personal growth: The conventional way of doing things and being in the world might not work now, so allow yourself to shift perspectives. If you dare to embrace change, Uranus might push you forward and even surprise you!

5. Develop your intuition by opening your third eye: Uranus is a planet of psychic abilities, so this is an opportunity to develop them. You will know Uranian brilliance is trying to arrive whenever you feel anxious or have flashes of insight.

Strategies for Harnessing Your Uranus Trines
Ages: 28 to 30, 55 to 57
The Waxing Uranus Trine (the first of two), happening between twenty-eight and thirty years old, is a time of life changes, especially because it overlaps with your First Saturn Return. The second one (Waning Uranus Trine), occurs a few years before your Second Saturn Return (59) and brings the opportunity to seek change without experiencing extreme disruption. Here are some tips:

1. Age 29: You're heading into a new decade, so take some time to think about the emerging views of the world around you, leaving room for more personal independence.
2. Age 29: Reconsider if the values of the social groups you belong to still resonate with you. If they don't, start making room for newer people to come into your life.
3. Age 56: You might feel a strong desire to break free from your profession now, choosing to retire early or transition to work that gives you more freedom.
4. Age 56: If a marriage or relationship has been feeling suffocating to you, this is a time to address it—either by changing its terms or ending it.
5. Age 56: Ask yourself if your life has been fulfilling up until now and make course-corrections.

Strategies for Navigating Your Uranus Opposition
Age: 39 to 45
Your Uranus Opposition—only happening once and lasting a whole year—is one of the most important and life-changing events in your life. This is what the term "midlife crisis" is made for, as it happens between your Saturn Return (twenty-nine years old) and your Chiron Return (fifty years old). Since Uranus is a planet of extremes whose energy flips like a switch, the effects are also extreme. Below is how to navigate both:

1. The first thing to do now is reconsider your relationship with Uranus. Remember, only 30 percent of the population seeks freedom to dance to the rhythm of their own drum. If you have repressed your desires due to any type of conditioning, this is when your inner switch might flip, pushing you to break free.

2. If you notice you have been unhappy with your career or marriage for some time, this would be a time to—hopefully less impulsively than not—make the necessary adjustments.

3. If you are within the 30 percent of the population who have remained faithful to their freedom-seeking values and desires, there might not be much to liberate you from, which means that this opposition would take you to exciting places! Like, for example, your intuition might take off, making you psychic (more about this in my personal Uranus Opposition story below).

4. Since Uranus is the planet of electricity, mental or corporal anxiety can be an effect now, manifesting as breakdowns or lack of sleep. Meditation, acupuncture, bodywork, and yoga (especially Kundalini yoga) are a must during this entire year.

5. Leave rigidity behind: Those with rigid minds and behaviors are the ones who struggle the most now. Even if being rigid (with yourself as well as others) has worked for most of your life, it might not work now. Strive to be more open-minded and understanding of change all around you.

Uranus Cycles: Personal Stories

In many cases and occasions, the effects of Uranus relate to a sense of newfound freedom. This was the case for Dick, a California-based entrepreneur and my dear father-in-law. Dick's story is not only interesting because he has lived long enough to experience his Uranus Return, which arrived when he was eighty-three years old. His Uranus story is one of liberation that links to a sweet love story, too.

After over a decade of being single, Dick met Dusya when he was eighty. They did not live in the same city, which means that to fully unite their lives, they would both have to move. Dick had owned a high-end art business for many years, which he would have to sell so he could focus on his new life with his bride. This wasn't easy for him, as he loves to work (his Jupiter is in Capricorn) and was deeply emotionally invested in what he did.

He ended up moving before selling the company, but in 2020, there was an even bigger sense of urgency to sell due to the global pandemic. In the summer of 2020, during the first activation of his Uranus Return, Dick began talking to potential buyers for his company. The process became long and tedious, with loads of prep and paperwork. After a lot of meetings and negotiation, Dick ended up selling his company two years later, once the third activation of his Uranus Return was totally over. By the summer of 2022, when he was soon to be eighty-five years old, he was finally liberated from work and fully ready to spend more time with his lovely wife.

MY URANUS OPPOSITION STORY

My Uranus Opposition story also involves liberation, as it was then when I finally decided to quit working as a senior astrologer for a big media company. Uranus helped me liberate myself from what I believed to be an industry in downfall and decadence. But at a deeper level, it was about becoming psychic and developing my intuition. A few months before my Uranus Opposition began, I started feeling a deep call to work with the Akashic Records. I could almost hear a voice guiding me to find out more about them and, by the spring of 2023, I had signed up for a six-month training to learn how to read them professionally.

The training ended up being way more intense than I had anticipated, as it was taking me on a deep path of healing and self-discovery, via the remembrance of my past lives. Without knowing it, I was beginning to develop my ability to communicate with angels, spirit guides, and my ancestors as well as other people's ancestors. The entire journey was magical and prepared me for one of the most transformative times in my life.

For many of us, Uranus activations end up being about awakening our intuition and opening the chakras, which are the conduit for Kundalini energy to move through the body. My Uranus Opposition ended in the spring of 2024, but what I built—my connection with my intuition and spirit guides—remains strong in my life.

Neptune

Keywords

Transcendence, Oneness, Compassion, Inspiration,
Glamour, Imagination, Spirituality, Vision, Psychic
Sensitivity, Dissolution, Fantasy, Delusion,
Addiction, Boundaryless, Loss

Neptune Archetypes

The Visionary, The Artist, The Mystic, The Dreamer,
The Guru, The Martyr

The Astronomy of Neptune

Neptune was the first planet discovered through mathematical calculations, back in 1846. This fact forever gave Neptune its oceanic nature, as ancient sailors navigated Earth's waters via the use of mathematical measurements of constellations. Dark and icy, Neptune lacks a solid surface—and scientists even believe that under its cold clouds, there could be an ocean of superhot water locked inside as well as massive diamond rains!

The planet is named after Neptune, the Roman god of fresh water, identified as Poseidon, (its Greek counterpart). According to more ancient myths, however, Poseidon was originally not a sea god. Poseidon's relationship with water originally came from his amorous relationships with female water goddesses such as Thetis and Amphitrite. For example, British astrologer Jessica Adams affirms that Poseidon's legendary trident was borrowed from Amphitrite, with whom he had a romance.

Neptunian things such as oceans, water, clouds, romance, and diamonds feel oh so rosy and romantic. But there is a lot about Neptune that is not what it seems. Overall, Neptune's astronomical mystery manifests in mythological—and real-life confusion—as you're about to see.

The Astrology of Neptune

To understand Neptune's astrological influence, it's crucial to remember the rulership of this planet over everything that is intangible. Everything that you can't either touch or see but that you can *feel* goes under its umbrella. Neptune is the ultimate spiritual influence, as it is connected to divine transcendence, which in many mystery schools means "reaching nirvana"—that magical state of bliss that goes beyond space and time.

Due to its subtle, intangible nature, it is fair to say that Neptune is the hardest planet to understand. This is especially true for those of us living in the West or within a culture that has ignored, suppressed, or manipulated a connection with Spirit. In my work as both an astrologer and an Akashic Channel, I've noticed it is this disconnection from Spirit that eventually leads to us experiencing the darker side of Neptune. The belief that only the tangible is real is what creates confusion, delusion, and even addiction.

Neptune's Lower Vibration

Neptune's astrological influence is one of the most polarized there is. We experience its lower vibration when we're trying to escape reality at all costs, often searching for something to numb us. Since Neptune is connected to higher states of consciousness, if we don't experience them naturally, we seek them through drugs, alcohol, and other addictive substances. It's as if we were under a spell, constantly repressing our search for real meaning in life.

Other manifestations of Neptune's lower vibration are lies and deceptions, some of which we tell ourselves. We believe someone else's manipulation (or our own) and are afraid of taking off the rose-colored glasses. Neptune's glamourized, hypnotizing effect on us is obvious to everyone else around us—except us! We want to see what we want to see, instead of what *is* real.

Those of us with Pisces Sun, Moon or Rising, Pisces South Node, Neptune in the first house, or Neptune at an angle need to work harder at managing its activations.

Embodying Neptune's Higher Vibration

At its highest vibration, Neptune is the planet of *vision*, which can be accessed via creative visualization. Think of Neptune as the planet that rules screens, cinematography, and vision boards. Neptune says: If you can truly visualize it, you can manifest it.

All accomplished photographers, musicians, painters, designers, and moviemakers have managed to harness Neptune's immense inspiration.

Another higher manifestation of Neptune comes as deep spiritual work. During Neptune activations, we're invited to explore the world of mysticism, meditation, and psychic energy. These practices deepen our inner life access, helping us develop a stronger connection with ourselves, the planets, and the universe. As esoteric as it might sound, Neptune is the planet that teaches us universal oneness: the awareness that we are all coming from the same source and are eventually returning to it.

Finding Your Neptune Sign

In your birth chart, your Neptune sign speaks of how you approach the world of dreams, imagination, spirituality, inspiration, and compassion. However, it will also be very telling of your blind spots.

Like Uranus, Neptune is a generational planet; you share the same Neptune sign as most people your age. To find your Neptune sign, enter your exact day and time of birth in my calculator: www.naramon.com/birth-chart-calculator. Once you find it, read about your way to approach the most subtle and magical of all planets.

Your Neptune Sign, Explained

Neptune in Aries

Having Neptune in Aries gives you amazing focus and resilience when it comes to manifesting and actualizing your dreams. A strong sense of intuition can also be yours if you truly learn to develop it and work with it. Otherwise, your mind could play tricks with you, making you feel like some people are out to get you when they really aren't and setting you off on never-ending fights that could be unnecessary. Learning to wait so you can truly break through clouds of confusion is one of your biggest life lessons.

Neptune in Taurus

Due to Neptune's snail-pace, the planet of magic hasn't visited Taurus since 1889. This means that no one alive has this combination, which will not start changing until 2038. This planet-sign combination is the epitome of creative finesse, ideal for working with artistic self-expression, especially singing and painting. The learning with this placement presents itself as balancing the search for material gain with spiritual development. In the end, what Neptune seeks is to unplug you from having a too-materialistic view of the world.

Neptune in Gemini

Neptune has not visited Gemini since 1902 and will not do so until 2051. Since Gemini rules communication and the written word, this is the combination that would create a flowery writer or someone with an innate gift for healing with words. You live life through the absorption of information and are in tune with media and mass consciousness. However, you must practice discernment due to Neptune's foggy influence, which at times could bring paranoia or information overload.

Neptune in Cancer

Neptune last visited Cancer in 1916 and will not return to the sign of the Crab until 2078. Since Cancer is the sign of family, those with this combination are likely to come from non-traditional households. Or perhaps there's also a lack of boundaries regarding space or roles within the family dynamics due to addiction or loss. Once these are healed and you find your true clan or tribe, this combination unlocks a deep sense of compassion to help others.

Neptune in Leo

As I write this book, few of us have this combination. Neptune was last in Leo in 1929 and will not return to this sign until 2078. Due to its connection with solar creativity, Leo is one of the best landscapes for Neptune to work its magic. This is a performative, flashy, and bold combination that plays with the power of images—think old-school Hollywood glamour! The only pitfall with this combination would be egocentrism without even realizing it.

Neptune in Virgo

Being born with this planet-sign combination means you're into simplicity and purity and are able to find beauty even in the mundane. You have a special talent for all things holistic, like herbal medicine and energy healing, and a special connection with the earth element, needing to spend time alone in nature whenever life gets stressful. Part of your journey involves being of service to society—but because oceanic Neptune knows no boundaries, it's crucial that you perform this without falling into self-sacrificing tendencies.

Neptune in Libra

Having Neptune in Libra means you are a true peacemaker, but you're also idealistic about your relationships. In your desire to merge with others, you're quick to ignore boundaries and red flags. In the end, every one of your closest relationships (especially romantic) has an evolutionary lesson for you. You're charming, poetic, and artistic, and you harness the gifts of this planet-sign combination through creativity pursuits such as design, videomaking, and fashion.

Neptune in Scorpio

Incredibly psychic, you're able to read people almost automatically. One of your deepest desires is to truly merge with someone and find true intimacy, but it's crucial to not confuse love with sacrifice. Having healthy boundaries might be one of your biggest lessons in life, especially when it comes to carrying other people's burdens (or the burdens of the world). Once you learn how to set boundaries and manage your psychic power and magnetism, the sky's the limit.

Neptune in Sagittarius

Having Neptune in Sagittarius means you are an explorer—physically, mentally, and spiritually. A forever scholar of life, you desire to know it all and are the happiest when allowing your mind to travel. However, avoid exploration and travel for the sake of escaping reality. Your impulsivity is exciting to those around you, but it can also take you down if you allow yourself to chase endlessly after fantasies. A highly spiritual old soul, you might even become a guru or teacher.

Neptune in Capricorn

You have a very serious approach to the world of the unseen (spirituality, dreams, and mysticism), which can sometimes prevent you from connecting with Spirit. But once you figure out that the magic is truly real, you're serious about aligning with it to manifest your dreams. Since you believe that an ideal world needs strong rules and regulations, it's part of your journey to help change the system from within. And while it might seem like your creativity might not mix well with your career, it's actually the other way around!

Neptune in Aquarius

You are an idealist and are not afraid to admit your strong belief in individuality, freedom, and collective activism. Not afraid of asking the tough questions about humanity, the world, and the universe, you're curious and open-minded. For you, it's vital to make a contribution to society, as you're very in tune with mass consciousness. But to be able to put your amazing capabilities to work, you must find the balance between what your mind and your heart tell you.

Neptune in Pisces

In modern astrology, Neptune is the natural ruler of Pisces, which means you have a very strong Neptune! You are a dreamer, full of imagination, intuition, and artistic abilities. These powers, if not harnessed, however, could easily turn into escapism. A truly sensitive being, you need time alone to recharge, as well as energetic protection from the outside world. Visualization is both your best friend when spending time in crowds and your ally when it comes to manifesting your dream life.

YOUR NEPTUNE CYCLE

Note: Your Neptune probably won't be in this position within your chart. What this illustration seeks to convey is how your Neptune cycle works. However, it does not include retrogrades, as each retrograde of Neptune is unique, bringing a different flavor each time.

One of the best things you can do for yourself and your peace of mind is keeping track of your Neptune activations. Why? Due to Neptune's nature, these tend to bring confusion, even the positive ones (the Sextile and Trine). Even when trying to pinpoint them, Neptune cycles are hard to spot—we simply fall into a nebulous state and mindset, making it difficult to remember things. On a more positive note, all Neptune activations can be highly spiritual and creative times in our lives.

To get even more specific dates regarding your current (or next) Neptune activations, head to this page: www.naramon.com/written-in-your-stars. Then match the results with the text below.

Strategies for Harnessing Your Neptune Sextile
Ages: 26 to 28

This is a mind and consciousness expansive activation. You're about to come into adulthood (your Saturn return) and are realizing the many opportunities in front of you. To make the best of it:

1. Reconnect with your dreams: There are many directions you could take; begin walking toward the one that seems more aligned with what your soul craves.

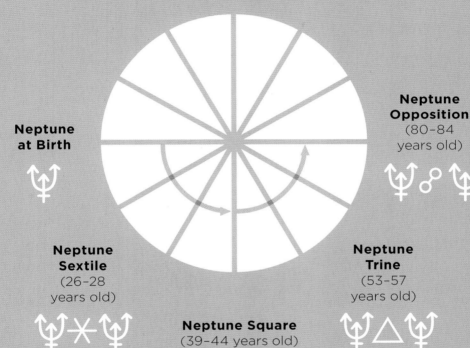

Neptune at Birth

Neptune Opposition
(80–84 years old)

Neptune Sextile
(26–28 years old)

Neptune Square
(39–44 years old)

Neptune Trine
(53–57 years old)

2. Explore your inner world: The mystical side of life will appeal to you—explore it, but keep your mind open to all practices, theories, and ways of approaching the richness of the world of the "unseen."

3. Dare to enter the mystery: Neptune transits, in general, instigate altered states of consciousness. Seek to find these through meditation, visualization, and learning magic or other esoteric practices.

4. Explore your creativity: Your imagination is heightened now, giving you access to inspiration coming from above. Harness it by exploring and developing artistic, poetic, or vibrant ideas that arrive.

5. Embrace self-compassion: A deeper understanding of yourself and your place in the universe is developing now, even if it's subtly. This involves accepting yourself as you are, without judging your imperfections.

Strategies for Navigating Your Neptune Square
Ages: 39 to 44
Your Neptune square is by far the most important part of the entire Neptune cycle for two reasons. First, it happens only once in your life. Second, it kicks off your "midlife crisis" cycles, paving the way for the Second Saturn Opposition and the Uranus Opposition. The Neptune Square is a time of confusion, when you begin questioning a lot of things regarding the direction of your life. Here are some tips to navigate it:

1. Go within: Since the square is an aspect of crisis and tension, you might wake up to some hard truths now. Because Neptune rules "the ideal," you might realize you are turning forty and perhaps are not yet "where you thought you would be." Shifting your focus from outward to inward is necessary now to align with what you truly want and not what you "think" you want.

2. Take note of your insights: Visions, ideas, and insights will arrive now—especially via dreams. These ideas might be brilliant—or not. Write them down so you can consider them when this activation is over.

3. Avoid big changes or permanent commitments: Since Neptune does not bring a decision-making type of energy, avoid quitting your job or ending a relationship until this activation is over. Observe rather than acting.

4. Deepen your sense of spirituality: Beginning a daily meditation practice is key now to allow yourself to explore the intangible side of life.

Strategies for Harnessing Your Neptune Trine
Ages: 53 to 57

All Neptune activations have a spiritual feel to them—especially this one! By this time, we have mastered the material world, and our focus turns more toward the nonmaterial part of life. This is the highest vibration of Neptune, which rules: imagination, compassion, and unity. Here are some tips:

1. Examine your life: From a compassionate approach, ask yourself if you have lived up to your deepest desires. If there is still a dream on your bucket list that you didn't get the chance to explore, this is the time to do so!

2. Explore creativity: Even if you never thought of yourself as a creative mind, you might find yourself interested in painting, photography, or poetry. Exposing yourself to art is also rewarding at this time.

3. Spread empathy: During this year, your degree of sensitivity to the external world is heightened, allowing you to connect with others at a deeper level. Joining a like-minded group could open doors for you.

4. Practice selflessness: Since you are feeling more compassionate, donating your time and effort to a greater cause could bring enormous satisfaction.

Strategies for Navigating Your Neptune Opposition
Ages: 80 to 84

This unique and rare activation of Neptune is mainly about letting go and serves as preparation for your Uranus Opposition, which arrives at 84. Astrologically speaking, the opposition is an aspect that requires *balance.* Here are some tips:

1. Let go of rigid views: The world is changing around you and some emerging views will be vastly different from yours. Replacing your old with new ways of thinking now sets you up for success and avoids confusion later on.
2. Embrace abstraction, spirituality, and rest: At this age, you are naturally less active, which enhances your senses and your inner life. Watch those movies you wanted to see. Read the books still on your list. And explore those "new age" practices you might have thought "were not for you."
3. Forgive and forget: You're at the end of your life and have made it all the way here! If you feel like you still need to let an old grudge go, that time is now!

Neptune Cycles: Personal Stories

Divine feminine coach and content creator Jillian Guerin has a magnificent Neptune sextile story. She was born with a Sun-Neptune opposition in her chart, which in some cases translates into either permanent or sporadic low immune systems. But the masterful way she would handle this part of her chart would change her life's trajectory!

When Jillian's Neptune was being activated by transits back when she was twenty-four, she began developing an auto-immune disease that made it difficult for her to show up to her corporate job. One year later, she resigned with the intention of going inward to focus on healing and finding herself.

During this inward and soul-searching process, Jillian experienced her Neptune sextile (for a total of three times, between 2018 and 2021). As someone who astrologers would call "a highly Neptunian individual," she had always enjoyed taking pictures and playing around with cameras from an early age. (Remember: Neptune is the planetary ruler of vision, screens, and movies.)

In between her first and second Neptune sextile activations, Jillian's visionary skills gave birth to the idea of launching a YouTube channel. After she experienced her exact third Neptune sextile activation, her Neptunian magic took a tangible turn when she published her first YouTube video in the fall of 2020. While watching her videos (her YouTube handle is @JillzGuerin), you will notice a hypnotizing aura about Jillian that encapsulates the phenomenon of divine feminine rising within our society and culture.

Four years later, Jillian has produced more than two hundred high-quality videos, gaining her over 500,000 followers and over 25 million views. In addition, while she was conceptualizing how to bring her vision to reality, her auto-immune issue began to resolve itself.

Pluto

Keywords
Birth-Death-Rebirth, Psychoanalysis,
Transmutation, Power, Regeneration, Eroticism,
Obsession, Darkness, Taboo, Manipulation,
Destruction, Jealousy, Vengeance, Evolution

Pluto Archetypes
The Phoenix, The Shaman, The Alchemist,
The Psychologist, The Ruler, The Tyrant

The Astronomy of Pluto

You've read how the discovery of Uranus revolutionized space exploration and how Neptune's first sighting elevated the importance of mathematics. Now, you get to find out how the discovery of Pluto forever changed how we humans relate to the deepest part of ourselves and our overall existence.

Discovered in 1930 in the distant Kuiper Belt, Pluto was first thought to be a planet. After all, its orbit contains those of all other eight planets. Due to its astronomical complexity and the discovery of other similar planetary bodies, Pluto was demoted to Dwarf Planet in 2006. This demotion should never drive us to believe less of Pluto, however. The fact that Pluto is small in comparison to other planets is not proportional to its immense power.

Tiny but mighty Pluto orbits incredibly far from the Sun, floating in a dark, hidden, and cold area of our solar system. This is a fact to pay attention to, as it relates to the immense meaning and effect that Pluto has in our lives. Pluto was discovered and came into our consciousness during a tumultuous time for humanity—as fascism was spreading across the globe and the destructive capabilities of atomic power were harnessed. On the other spectrum, Pluto's discovery coincided with the shaping of psychology and psychotherapy as self-discovery and healing practices.

The Astrology of Pluto

Pluto was named after the Roman god of the underworld, and many think of the Greek god Hades as its counterpart. However, the Plutonian archetype existed in human consciousness way before that! As astrologer and historian Richard Tarnas puts it, "Pluto is the dark, mysterious, taboo, and often terrifying reality that lurks beneath the surface of things. Pluto impels, burns, consumes, transfigures, resurrects. In mythic and religious terms, it is associated with all myths of descent and transformation, and with all deities of destruction and regeneration, death and rebirth: Dyonysius, Hades and Persephone, Pan, Medusa, Lilith, Inanna, Isis and Osiris, the volcano goddess Pele, Quetzalcoatl, Kundalini, Shiva, Kali, Shakti."

If Saturn teaches, Uranus liberates, and Neptune dissolves, Pluto transforms. Its job is to expose what's hidden so we can process it and alchemize it into something new and more powerful. In your birth chart, your Pluto placement by house and sign depicts the darker sides of your journey, your trauma, and the shadow material that you might have even carried with you from a past life to this incarnation. Pluto's influence runs deep, and while everyone experiences it to a certain degree, it is not your classic dinner table conversation.

Pluto's Lower Vibration

Pluto is also a planet of extremes. At its worst, Pluto activations can be manipulative, secretive, vengeful, or self-destructive. Since Pluto correlates to the entire concept of control, we're under its darker side whenever we're exerting it on others or falling victim to it. We either become the tyrant or fall prey to one, stuck in intense power dynamics.

Control goes hand in hand with obsession and the need to manipulate those around us due to a fixation on a desired outcome. This obsession and desire for control tap into a deep part of ourselves—the subconscious mind—with its roots in traumatic experiences.

When we're exhibiting Pluto's lower vibration, we avoid accepting, seeing, and tending to our trauma, which can eventually led to its repetition. Astrologers see the darker side of Pluto at play over and over again when it comes to patterns of abuse. If a person experiences abuse during childhood and never attempts to face it, this pattern often repeats in adulthood.

Embodying Pluto's Higher Vibration

Pluto is the planetary vehicle of the natural "Law of Energy"—it is neither created nor destroyed; it can only transmute. Pluto gives us a choice: to avoid our shadow and re-live it, or to alchemize it into personal power.

Embodying Pluto's higher vibration is not easy as, in some cases, it can feel like experiencing a "dark night of the soul." Responding to Pluto's activations requires us to excavate deep inside ourselves, getting to the heart of the matter. It's like digging a hole in the sand, looking for a treasure that is hidden at the very bottom of our subconscious mind. It can be a long process. But once we have surrendered to the transformation, we soar like the phoenix rising. This is how shamans and witches become powerful agents of transformation for others; they must first face their dark side, accept it, even love it, and then alchemize it into a unique strength put to the service of others.

Finding Your Pluto Sign

Like Uranus and Neptune, Pluto is a generational planet, so it should be easy to find your Pluto sign. Those of us who have planets in Scorpio, as well as Pluto connecting with the Sun, Moon, Venus, Mars, or Pluto at an angle as well as Pluto in the First or Seventh Houses, know this planet's energy well. We are survivors turned powerful catalysts for positive change!

To find your Pluto sign, enter your exact day and time of birth in my calculator: www.naramon.com/birth-chart-calculator. Due to Pluto's eccentric orbit (more on this on pages 117 and 118), you will most likely have Pluto in either Libra, Scorpio, Sagittarius, or Capricorn.

Your Pluto Sign, Explained

Pluto in Aries

The last time Pluto visited Aries was in 1852, so no one alive has this Pluto sign. The next humans with Pluto in Aries will arrive starting in 2068. Aries is a fire sign, ruling over courage, ambition, and passionate bravery. Since Pluto intensifies everything that it touches, this would be a volatile combination. At its worst, it would deal with violence—and at its best, it would constantly fight to achieve freedom and a true sense of individuality.

Pluto in Taurus

The last time someone was born with Pluto in Taurus was 1884, and the next time this happens will be 2096. For this reason, astrologers don't really know how this planet-sign combination would manifest at a personal level. However, this would be a generation that would experience Pluto's transformative effects when it comes to beauty, money, property, resources, and personal values. People with this combination would witness extremes in wealth, whether they are very rich or very poor.

Pluto in Gemini

Pluto hasn't visited the sign of the Twins since 1914, so very few people have this combination. For this generation, "the power of the mind" was elevated to a new level, as they witnessed all things communication (phone, radio, mass media) going mainstream. With this planet-sign combination, Pluto's obsessive tendency fixates on having all the facts, figures, and knowledge. Therefore, learning how to balance the intake and synthesis of information was ever so important. If you obsess too much with information and are constantly going down rabbit holes to search for the answers, it can be detrimental to the psyche and sense of intellectual wellbeing.

Pluto in Cancer

As of 2024, the generation born between 1914 and 1938 is the oldest generation alive! Since Cancer is the only zodiac sign ruled by the Moon, which relates to nurturance and food, this was the first generation that experienced the concept of "canned food." The shadow side of this generation manifested as the silencing of "what really was going on at home." Maternal and caretaking instincts were forever changed by this generation, as this is when the world first started noticing the misalignment in gender roles.

Pluto in Leo

If you have Pluto in Leo, you are part of the "baby boomer" generation. Since Pluto rules extremes as well as the shadow, this can be either a positively powerful or an ultimately destructive combination. Its highest vibration manifests as magnanimous creativity that constantly transforms and evolves, and that truly comes from the heart. Its shadow side tends to manifest as massive ego trips and entitlement, with the delusion of always being right or deserving to have everything that one could possibly desire.

Pluto in Virgo

Having the planet of transformation in Virgo means your power comes in noticing all the details, especially those that very few notice. You want to fix, refine, and perfect things, processes, and most likely people as well—but you must avoid this fixation that would lead you to cross other people's boundaries. Channeled correctly, this combination can do wonders when it comes to developing alternative and natural healing modalities. Its service-oriented nature could also be about cleaning Earth's pollution. After all, this is the flower-power generation that gave birth to Greenpeace.

Pluto in Libra

If your Pluto sign is Libra, you are meant to experience personal transformation through your relationships. Extreme—really empowering or really intense—experiences might be present in your life, sometimes bringing a sense of social exhaustion. Your relationships are your mirrors and means for personal evolution, so one of your key lessons in this incarnation is to feel empowered by your connections without losing sight of your own sense of identity. The fight for creating justice, harmony, and equality for all is one of your generation's staples.

Pluto in Scorpio

Scorpio is one of the strongest signs for Pluto, so if you have this combination, you were born during a time of intense societal transformation. Your generation (millennials) was tasked with transforming the way we see and approach sex, intimacy, feelings, and power dynamics. You learn and evolve by acknowledging your deep need for control, especially when it comes to emotionally charged scenarios and situations. Part of your journey also involves airing out what other generations have repressed, leading humanity toward a true sense of healing.

Pluto in Sagittarius

Sagittarius is a sign that deals with knowledge, philosophy, and faith—so you were born with an extreme desire to transform that. You constantly question what others take as "written" or "fact," needing to create your philosophy of life—which, by the way, is set to always transform and evolve. Without this desire to challenge the mental status quo, some people with this combination can fall prey to acquiring extreme points of view or even religions. Pluto in Sagittarius is a sure call to "become your own guru."

Pluto in Capricorn

Capricorn deals with our foundational life processes, such as career, family, and the government. Your generation was tasked with, slowly but surely, transforming all of that. And in 2020, when Pluto hit its climax of activation in the sky, the whole concept of business and career was forever changed with virtual and online work becoming prevalent. You are a silent type of maverick, preferring to change the world from a strategic place and mindset. Incredibly ambitious, you're better off balancing work and play to keep your life full and lighthearted. Otherwise, burnout and loneliness can easily creep into your life.

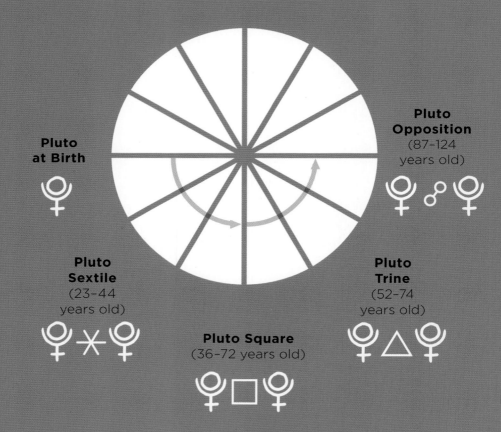

Pluto at Birth

♇

Pluto Opposition (87–124 years old)

♇ ⚬ ♇

Pluto Sextile (23–44 years old)

♇ ✶ ♇

Pluto Trine (52–74 years old)

♇ △ ♇

Pluto Square (36–72 years old)

♇ □ ♇

Pluto in Aquarius

As I am writing this book, in the summer of 2024, newborn babies are being born with this planet-sign combination, which is something that hasn't happened since 1797. Pluto will be in Aquarius for twenty years (2023 to 2044), creating a long generation tasked with taking humanity from the old traditional ways into the new era, also known as the Age of Light or the Age of Aquarius. This is expected to be an innovative, inventive, rebellious, and progressive generation that will fight for the right to be free, different, and empowered.

Pluto in Pisces

The last time someone was born with this combination was 1822, and the next time will not be until 2044. Pisces zodiac sign rules spirituality, mysticism, music, art, and the oceans—so this will be a generation that will greatly transform all that. This generation will be one of immense creativity and creation—which, if untapped, may lead to escapism or addiction. In addition, this generation will need to be intuitive when finding their place in the world and the universe at large.

YOUR PLUTO CYCLE

Note: Your Pluto probably won't be in this position within your chart. What this illustration seeks to convey is how your Pluto cycle works. However, it does not include retrogrades, as each retrograde of Pluto is unique, bringing a different flavor each time.

Dwarf planet Pluto has an eccentric orbit, meaning that it does not spend the same amount of time in each one of the signs. For example, we know Jupiter spends about a year in each sign, from Aries to Pisces, and Neptune spends thirteen years in each sign. Pluto does not have this same behavior. Due to its elliptical orbit (248 years around the Sun), Pluto spends the least amount of time in Scorpio (fourteen years) and the longest time in Taurus (thirty-one years). For this reason, the time range of Plutonian activations varies much more from generation to generation.

For example, I was born with Pluto in Libra and experienced my Pluto sextile at twenty-five years old. This means that my generation experiences life faster than the younger generations. As of 2024, those who were born with Pluto at the very last degrees of Cancer are currently experiencing their Pluto Opposition (Pluto at the very last degree of Capricorn). At the time of this publication, the oldest person alive (born with Pluto in Gemini) is 117 years old; she experienced her Pluto Opposition (Pluto in Sagittarius) when she was 97 years old.

But this is not the case for everyone. As I write this, newborn babies will have their Pluto in Aquarius and will experience their Pluto sextile (their first Pluto-Pluto activation) at forty-three years old and the Pluto Square at seventy-two years old. The Pluto in Aquarius generation will not experience either the Pluto Trine or the Pluto Opposition.

To get even more specific dates regarding your current (or next) Pluto activations, head to this page: www.naramon.com/written-in-your-stars, then match the results with the text below.

Strategies for Navigating Your Pluto Sextile
Ages: 23 to 44
The Pluto sextile is a key activation to pay attention to, as it is the first Pluto-Pluto activation we experience in life. This is a time of great empowerment, when we become aware of the great possibilities that lie ahead of us. Below is how to make the best of it:

1. Explore the concept of power: Reflect on the way you will exert your personal power in the world, which will be colored by your Pluto sign and astrological house.
2. Cultivate deep relationships: Fascinating people will enter your life now, and they are here to teach you about owning your power and chasing your dreams.
3. Embrace the mysteries of life: Pluto rules research, so this is a wonderful time to dive into anything that fascinates you but that you don't yet know about. Astrology, magic, psychology, and all things "hidden" or "taboo" might fascinate you.
4. Chase your passions: The practices or habits that come into your life now could become long-term, so pay attention to them. When I had my Pluto sextile at twenty-five years old, I went to Europe for the first time, which was a mind-opening experience. Ever since, traveling to new countries has become one of my priorities. This makes sense, because I have three planets in Sagittarius, the sign of traveling and exploration.

Strategies for Navigating Your Pluto Square
Ages: 36 to 72

The Pluto Square can be either one of the most destructive or potent of your life—it all depends on how you handle it! During this twelve- to eighteen-month period, the planetary Alchemist, Pluto seeks to regenerate something in your life, transforming old energy into something new. It will do so by exposing what seems to be lifeless or already dead in your life. Below is how to respond to it:

1. Allow for the past to fade away: Whether it is a job, a relationship, or a habit, Pluto will destroy what is no longer meant to stay in your life. The word "trust" is a big one now, and you should trust that, eventually, what is going away will be replaced by something new.
2. Reevaluate the overall direction of your life: If you're not living to your higher potential, Pluto will show it to you by bringing moments of psychological crisis. This would be a productive time to work with a therapist or coach to evaluate your life goals and focus.
3. Navigate power struggles with care and awareness: Two types of people are likely to challenge you now: those who are resisting your evolution, and those who are showing you the way toward it. As friendly as possible, ignore the first type and invest more of your time and energy listening to the second group.

Strategies for Navigating Your Pluto Trine
Ages: 52 to 74

If you are from the Pluto in Leo, Virgo, and Libra generations, this activation occurs during your fifties or early sixties. If you are from the Pluto in Scorpio or Sagittarius generation, you will experience this activation during your seventies or eighties.

In astrology, the Trine is an aspect of ease, but since Pluto is the most transformative planet, its effects are felt more intensely. Here are some tips:

1. Embrace deep reflection: What is truly meaningful for you? Once you find out, invest your time and energy in that.
2. Perform a cleansing of your life: Take inventory of possessions, relationships, and habits and resolve to get rid of the ones that no longer bring value to your life or that are no longer useful.

3. Uncover subconscious patterns: If you've fallen into negative habits, this activation can help you shed light on them as well as how to overcome them.
4. Seek power in numbers: Chat about this process with people who are the same age as you; they are experiencing the same opportunity to create conscious awareness.

Strategies for Navigating Your Pluto Opposition
Ages: 87 to 124

Not everyone (only those born in the middle of the twentieth century) will experience this Pluto activation, and those who do will be in their eighties when it happens. Since Pluto tends to expose what was previously hidden, what could be an end-of-life activation uncovers a great deal of psychological material about one's life. But due to the opposition being an aspect of tension, the Pluto Opposition is about balancing the full spectrum of emotions that arises now. Here are some tips.

1. Accepting change and transformation: You might be wondering; "this type of change, at my age?" The answer is yes! Regardless of its nature, welcome it, as going against it will only make things more difficult for you and those around you.
2. Right your wrongs: Pluto is the planet of power, so if you exerted or mismanaged yours throughout your life, a true sense of remorse could suddenly translate into sleepless nights. It's never too late to apologize or to take an "actions speak louder than words" approach to amends.
3. Align with the times: Study, read, and go deep into the challenges facing the new generations. This will give you a well-rounded view of the current state of the world.

PLUTO CYCLES: PERSONAL STORIES

My husband and partner Alex Drossler has a fascinating Pluto Square story that I want to share in the spirit of proving to you the immense power Pluto can convey in our lives. Alex was born with Pluto in Libra in the 10th house, meaning that one of his life's themes is about developing his personal power in the realm of career.

When Pluto was traveling in Capricorn in 2020 and began forming a square with Alex's natal Pluto in Libra, he found himself at a critical juncture. He had spent over a decade working for his father's company in the high-end art industry, something he enjoyed but that was not his passion. By the summer of 2020, he had already earned a master's degree in aerospace engineering but was struggling to make the switch and find a job in this new field. He was having trouble unrooting from his family business to focus on what he truly wanted to do.

This was when the 2020 pandemic was hitting hard. We were living in San Francisco at that time when I brought Alex the idea to momentarily move to Mexico so he could truly focus on creating his new path. At first, he resisted it, but he ended up quitting his job, and we moved abroad! Three months later, he found what is still his current job as a director of mission design in the private aerospace industry sector. After living in four countries in one year (!), we came back to California and bought a house together. By the time his Pluto Square was over in 2022, he had a new career and owned his first home.

What Alex did took courage and risk-taking—after all, working for his dad meant having a certain degree of financial security. At a subconscious level, which is the level Pluto works at, he knew his old career was over and it was time to take the rest of his life into his own hands.

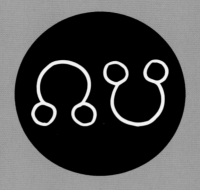

The Lunar Nodes

Keywords

The Soul's Journey, Karma, Reincarnation,
Past Lives, Destiny, Fate, Life Purpose, Past
Life Lessons, Evolution, Soul Ties, Karmic
Inheritance, Integration of Opposites,
Energy Cycle

The Astronomy of the Lunar Nodes

We've arrived at one of the most mesmerizing themes in astrology—the Lunar Nodes of Destiny. Also known as the Nodes of Fate, these mysterious archetypes are not physically breathing beings—unlike the planets, they are mathematical points in the sky. Simply put, the Lunar Nodes are the points of intersection between the apparent path of the Sun and the Moon's orbit around Earth.

Without even knowing the specifics, you've probably been exposed to the most visual manifestation of the nodes if you've been lucky enough to see an eclipse. When the luminaries (Sun and Moon) align with the nodes, we experience eclipses; both solar and lunar, two to three times a year.

There are two points marked, opposing one another, with the North Node being the Ascending Node and the South Node being the Descending Node. This means that the two nodes are always working together, facing each other, in opposite signs of the zodiac. For example, if the North Node is traveling in Gemini at any given time, the South Node will be traveling in the opposite sign of the zodiac wheel, which in this case is Sagittarius.

The nodes spend eighteen months in each zodiac axis, taking a full loop of the entire zodiac in about eighteen and a half years. Unlike the planets, the Lunar Nodes travel in retrograde motion, as they move clockwise, which is opposite to the Earth's own spin around the Sun. However, it's important to note that about once a month, the Lunar Nodes move in a direct, linear motion. This means that in rare cases, someone will have the nodes moving direct in their chart.

The Astrology of the Lunar Nodes

Fascinating and mesmerizing, the interpretation of the Lunar Nodes is one of my favorite topics and one I often use in my astrological and counseling practice. A visual that will help you tremendously when understanding how the Lunar Nodes work is to compare them to the Dragon greatly depicted in Chinese culture. The Dragon's head is the North Node, a point of intake, where the energy comes in. The Dragon's tail is the South Node, a point of outtake, where the energy goes out.

Judith Hill, in her book *The Lunar Nodes*, affirms that Vedic astrologers consider the Lunar North Node (Rahu) to be a point of *dharma* and, therefore, related to fame, prestige, and luck. Then, the Lunar South Node (Ketu) is a point of *karma*, bringing a focus on negative, addictive, and self-destructive tendencies.

Humanistic and modern approaches—like the one used by evolutionary astrology—are more about integrating the learnings from past lives (South Node or Ketu) into this incarnation (North Node of Rahu) to reach personal evolution in this lifetime. I take this approach with my clients, as I am a firm believer and explorer of the topic of past lives and reincarnation.

Harnessing Your Lunar Nodes

Evolving, in this lifetime, with your Lunar Node of Destiny requires a deep amount of awareness and self-observation. In my astrological practice, I have noticed most people still being stuck in their South Node (in their past), whenever coming for readings. Here's why: The zodiac sign the South Node occupies in your birth chart speaks of what your soul remembers from past lives. It's very informative of who you were, what your focus was, and what you did and learned in previous incarnations. For this reason, most of us tend to gravitate toward it, as it is what we remember and, therefore, what comes easily to us.

But as many esoteric traditions teach us, the main reason behind incarnation is to learn and evolve. What our soul truly wants is an overall balanced experience; it desires to learn the other side of the coin and, therefore, in this lifetime, it chooses the polar opposite sign experience. This is your North Node, your future, and what your soul yearns to absorb to become whole. However, the sign your North Node occupies is difficult because it is an energy you do not yet know. It is bound to feel uncomfortable—at least until you truly begin walking that path. Once you do, everything in life starts falling into place; life just begins happening *for* you!

Integrating Your Lunar Nodes

It's crucial to remember that finding your South Node sign is not about avoiding and hexing from your life everything that that sign means. Instead, it's about integrating your past energy into your future self. It is about harnessing the tools you acquired in the past to create a better, more aligned future.

To better understand how this works, I will share my story with you. I was born in the fall of 1979, so my destiny line falls in the Virgo-Pisces axis, with my South Node being in Pisces and my North Node being in Virgo. During my first astrology reading as a teen, I remember the reader telling me that my soul path was "being of service." To be completely honest, I was confused and puzzled by her statement. It wasn't until 2018, when I started studying astrology more seriously, that I realized what she meant.

In my previous incarnations, I had been a deeply spiritual person who spent a lot of time alone, accumulating a lot of mystical knowledge (Pisces). Therefore, in this incarnation, I am meant to bring that knowledge to society by writing about it and being of service by healing others (Virgo). My life changed when I discovered this—I stopped fantasizing about moving to Timbuktu and being a spiritual recluse, away from the troubles of the world. Writing isn't the easiest thing for me, but I know this is what I am meant to do to keep thriving in life.

Finding Your Nodal Axis

If you don't know your birth chart's nodal axis, you're in for a major discovery concerning your soul's journey, before and beyond this incarnation. Find your Lunar Nodes by entering your birth data in this link: www.naramon.com/birth-chart-calculator. Once found, read your North Node in the next section.

Disclaimer: If you are one of the rare people who were born with the nodes moving direct (rather than in retrograde motion), you would benefit greatly from exploring your past lives via regressions, the Akashic Records, or Family Constellations.

Your Nodal Nodes Explained

North Node in Aries/South Node in Libra
Move away from:
> co-dependency, indecision, debilitating self-lessness, and
> people-pleasing tendencies

You must cultivate:
> courage, independence, ambition toward your goals,
> and the "solo mentality"

In your past lives, you were the designer, the assistant, or the diplomat—
someone whose focus was on pushing someone else's vision. Therefore,
"making someone else happy" was truly necessary. In this incarnation,
you must learn to act, initiate, lead, and forge your own path without
worrying about others' desires or expectations. Also, having a regular
workout routine is a must!

North Node in Taurus/South Node in Scorpio
Move away from:
> control, obsession, a crisis mindset, emotional intensity

You must cultivate:
> patience, harmony, pleasure, financial freedom,
> a true sense of self-worth

In your past lives, you were involved in relationships with powerful people, which created a dynamic in which there were no boundaries when it
came to your emotional, financial, or sexual life. In this incarnation, you
must learn to have strict boundaries and the freedom to create your own
value system and financial resources. Building a strong connection to
the Earth is vital for your success.

North Node in Gemini/South Node in Sagittarius
Move away from:
> excess, dogma, careless optimism, careless spontaneity,
> self-righteousness

You must cultivate:
> logic, curiosity, tact, listening, intellectual pursuits,
> embracing dichotomy

In your past lives, your priority was to find either the absolute truth or nirvana itself! You did this by extensively exploring the world as well as many religions. In this incarnation, you must move away from dogma and develop your intellectual skills in other fields. All things communication—writing, speaking, podcasting, fact-checking, learning languages—are your path to finding yourself and your place in the world.

North Node in Cancer/South Node in Capricorn
Move away from:
> coldness, fear of intimacy, ignoring your feelings,
> excessive focus on success

You must cultivate:
> empathy, humility, emotional expression and depth,
> nurturance (for self and others)

In your past lives, you were in a position of power and authority, calling all the shots. You had to make important decisions and gave up precious time with yourself as well as your family. In this incarnation, a focus on building a strong family (or tribe) is critical for your evolution, as is finding a career that centers around nurturing others.

North Node in Leo/South Node in Aquarius
Move away from:
> aloofness, group mentality, emotional detachment,
> excessive search for knowledge

You must cultivate:
> creativity, individuality, risk-taking, self-confidence,
> leadership, a center-stage attitude

In your past lives, you were a group-focused scientist or intellectual, very concerned with having all the information before moving forward. In this incarnation, your journey is more about having fun and taking the risk of exploring your artistic abilities, without worrying so much about the public. The entrepreneurial journey is better for you than working for a corporation.

North Node in Virgo/South Node in Pisces
Move away from:
> self-doubt, escapism (drugs and alcohol), excessive daydreaming, a victim mentality

You must cultivate:
> order, moderation, routine, an analytical mind, healthy boundaries, a service-oriented mentality

In your past lives, you were a mystic and spiritualist—an extremely sensitive soul very attuned to other people's energies. You have arrived at this incarnation with incredibly healing powers—and you must put them to the service of others. A career in medicine or the holistic healing arts would be ideal, but this does not mean working for free or to your own detriment.

North Node in Libra/South Node in Aries
Move away from:
> anger, resentment, selfishness, impulsiveness, excessive self-assertion

You must cultivate:
> peace and harmony, diplomacy, balance, beautiful surroundings, win-win situations

You are a true survivor, as in your past lives as a warrior! For this reason, you come into this lifetime with a strong sense of individuality and self-sufficiency. Since you didn't get a chance to do this before, in this incarnation, you're meant to learn how to connect, relate to, and work with others in peace and harmony. You are meant to become a people person.

North Node in Scorpio/South Node in Taurus
Move away from:
> laziness, possessiveness, stubbornness, hedonism, materialism, addiction to food or sex

You must cultivate:
> self-inspection, emotional intelligence, constructive change, willingness to partner

You were pretty well-off in your past lives and for the most part, you got your way! Therefore, you came into this incarnation with an extremely rigid belief system. Embracing change is incredibly critical for your evolution, as is focusing less on the pleasures of life so you can, instead, find the psychological reasons why you (and others) do the things you do.

North Node in Sagittarius/South Node in Gemini

Move away from:

gossiping, drama, excessive curiosity or attachment to facts, unnecessary change

You must cultivate:

trust, exploration, world travel, a philosophical mindset, having a clear target

In your past lives, you were an intellectual (writer or teacher) who needed to accumulate facts and other people's opinions. Your mental energy was dispersed—therefore, you must now come in contact with your own truth, giving birth to your very own philosophy of life. To do this, you're invited to study subjective practices such as anthropology and philosophy.

North Node in Capricorn/South Node in Cancer

Move away from:

moodiness, insecurity, emotional manipulation, isolation, co-dependence

You must cultivate:

setting and achieving goals, self-control, a success mindset, letting go of the past

Your life was incredibly interconnected to your family or tribe in your past lives, which you most likely easily remember. In this lifetime, you must forge your own path, career, and goals without being overly concerned about what your tribe thinks of it. Setting your mind toward the future and achieving emotional, career, and financial freedom will help you grow and evolve.

North Node in Aquarius/South Node in Leo
Move away from:
>   selfishness, attention-seeking behaviors and fame, melodramatic
>   tendencies, stubbornness

You must cultivate:
>   objectivity, social equality, intellectual pursuits, a community-
>   oriented mentality

You were the actor, ballet dancer, or gifted performer in your past lives—
but this creative focus is no longer your soul path. To fully thrive, you
must move from a "me" to "us" mentality, as you have enormous contributions to bring to the world. As astrologer Judith Hill puts it, "contrib-
uting and enlightening mankind is your dharma," and the sooner you
begin walking this path, the happier you will be.

North Node in Pisces/South Node in Virgo
Move away from:
>   worry, anxiety, nervousness, attachment to facts, over-analysis,
>   compulsive tendencies

You must cultivate:
>   change, compassion, forgiveness, spiritual development, believing in
>   a higher power

In your past lives, you were a healer (nurse or doctor) and had a great
deal of responsibility. Without any room for mistakes, you became a perfectionist. In this lifetime, there isn't such a risk and, instead of worrying
so much, the universe invites you to just trust that you are being guided
by a higher power. You are meant to walk the spiritual, mystical path.

YOUR LUNAR NODES CYCLE
18.5 Years

Note: Your Lunar Nodes probably won't be in this position within your chart. What this illustration seeks to convey is how the entire cycle of your Lunar Nodes works.

On page 132 are the most important Nodal activations that everyone experiences at the approximate ages mentioned, with each one lasting for about six months. As you can see, the entire cycle adds up to 18.5 years. Your Nodal Returns, and secondly, the oppositions (both bolded) will always be more important and eventful. The Nodal Sextile and Trine is the easiest and most positive—and luckily, the one that happens the most! Unlike the planets, the Lunar Nodes are a combination, which means that the sextile and trines always come together.

To get even more specific dates regarding your current or future Lunar Nodes activations, head to this page: www.naramon.com/written-in-your-stars. Then match the results with the text below.

Strategies for Navigating Your Nodal Returns
Ages: 18, 37, 56, 74, 93

Your Nodal Return years are magical, as they are moments in time when you get to meet with your soul, the part of yourself that is timeless and never dies. This is when your destiny imprint repeats in the sky above, showing you the way forward as things in your life fall into place. Follow the steps below to maximize this sweet gift from the universe, as it won't repeat for another eighteen years!

1. Review your attachments to the past: The universal current of energy will show you where to go and where not to go. Pay attention to the signs and the subtle energies around you.
2. Explore your past lives: Via past life regressions or Akashic Records readings, invest time, energy, and effort in remembering the tools you acquired in previous incarnations (South Node) so you can invest them in finding success in this incarnation (North Node).
3. Inspect relationships: Masters, teachers, and mentors show up now to remind you of your cosmic imprint—of how you've always been, supporting you into becoming a new, more evolved version of yourself.

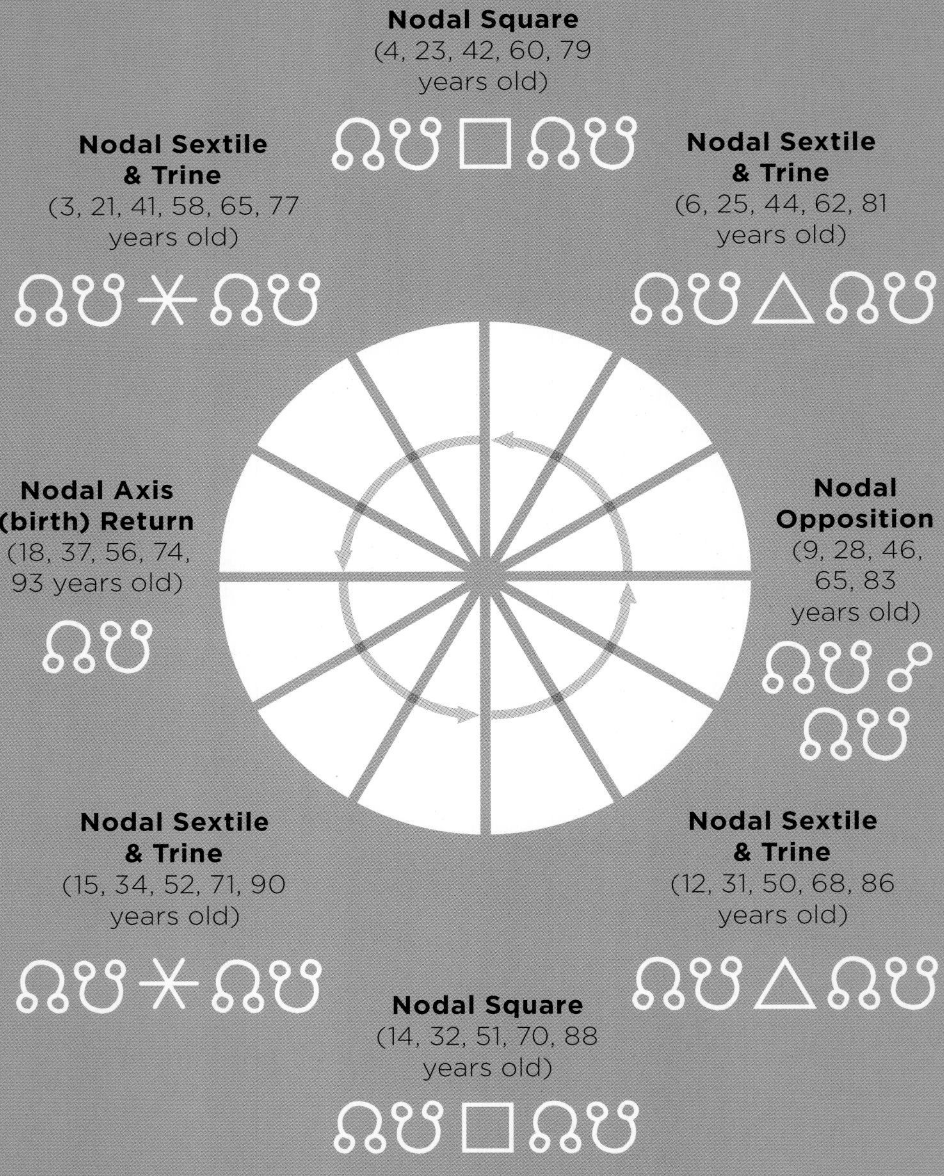

Nodal Square
(4, 23, 42, 60, 79 years old)

☊☋ □ ☊☋

Nodal Sextile & Trine
(3, 21, 41, 58, 65, 77 years old)

☊☋ ✶ ☊☋

Nodal Sextile & Trine
(6, 25, 44, 62, 81 years old)

☊☋ △ ☊☋

Nodal Axis (birth) Return
(18, 37, 56, 74, 93 years old)

☊☋

Nodal Opposition
(9, 28, 46, 65, 83 years old)

☊☋ ☍ ☊☋

Nodal Sextile & Trine
(15, 34, 52, 71, 90 years old)

☊☋ ✶ ☊☋

Nodal Sextile & Trine
(12, 31, 50, 68, 86 years old)

☊☋ △ ☊☋

Nodal Square
(14, 32, 51, 70, 88 years old)

☊☋ □ ☊☋

4. Try and test new things: This is when new talents might become latent, so stay open to new habits, practices, and hobbies that spark your interest. They could become something bigger down the road.

Strategies for Harnessing Your Nodal Sextiles and Trines
Ages: 3, 6, 12, 15, 21, 25, 31, 34, 41, 44, 50, 52, 58, 62, 68, 71, 77, 81, 86, 90

Your Nodal Sextiles and Trines, which go hand in hand, are opportunities to self-actualize with your soul, the deepest part of yourself. Destiny and fate are at play in the best way possible now, putting events and people along the way that will be crucial for both your success and your evolution. To make the best of them, you will have to create conscious awareness so these golden opportunities don't pass you by. Here are some tips:

1. Notice all the nuances: Signs are everywhere now and, yes, they are trying to tell you something. Don't discard anything and pay attention to every single little symbol, feeling, or thought that comes or repeats at a specific time.
2. Welcome new people into your orbit: Friends, teachers, gurus, and supporters suddenly and magically appear now to bring you exactly what you need to either make something happier or keep evolving. Many of these are, indeed, karmic connections with a beautiful story behind them.
3. Trust your timing: If your intuition is telling you this is the correct timing for something, follow it, even if logic doesn't seem to align with it. Both the universe and timing are on your side.
4. Feel positive about your future: The mantra "everything is happening for me" applies here, and the more you repeat it, the sweeter the blessings bound to come your way!

Strategies for Navigating Your Nodal Squares
Ages: 4, 14, 23, 32, 42, 51, 60, 70, 79, 88

Your Nodal Squares represent your ability to learn lessons either from past incarnations or what you need to overcome at a karmic level. In astrology, the square is an aspect of tension, so expect to feel it on the outside. But in the end, the lessons come at a very spiritual, deep level.

Whether you're ready or not, these are times to act and make decisions, as the universe will present you with choices. Here are some tips:

1. Choose wisely: Fate and destiny are at play now, bringing events that will ask you to make a tough choice between two paths: Your South Node (past) or North Node (future). What you choose now will take you either up or down! Spoiler alert: You're always better off choosing your North Node, your path of discomfort that eventually leads to enlightenment.

2. Practice extra self-care: Since these are months of energetic pressure, give your body, mind, and spirit extra love and care. It is in these moments of rest that you might receive that aha moment you so much need now.

3. Upgrade your filter: Part of the tension you feel now is the universe's way of getting you to wake up and open your eyes to the fact that the world is always changing. Ask yourself: How can I upgrade myself, my beliefs, and my toolkit to the changing times?

Strategies for Navigating Your Nodal Oppositions
Ages: 9, 28, 46, 65, 83

Your Nodal Oppositions—also called Reverse Nodal Returns—are major eye-opening moments along your journey. This is when the sky mirrors back your Nodal combination but in reversed motion; with the South Node (the Dragon's tail) activating your North Node (destiny point). Life can get a bit confusing during these six months, requiring you to make adjustments. The good news? You only have to face this specific challenge once every eighteen years. Here are some tips:

1. Unroot limiting beliefs: This is when your old behaviors, habits, and ways of seeing the world will be challenged. It's time to ask yourself: "Why do I do this or believe that?" Allow your family and societal preconditioning to fade away, as much as possible.

2. Inspect energetic blockages: Obstacles along the way occur now, as the universe is trying to get you to pay attention! Instead of going left, consider going right (and vice versa—even if it doesn't feel right).

3. Get out of your comfort zone: This is a time of major adjustments along your journey—so if you're still stuck in your South Node (past lives), this is your opportunity to make the switch. If you show courage to turn your life around, the universe will push you forward.

4. Dare to take U-turns: Some old ways will no longer work now, as you're being challenged to embrace what you normally wouldn't.

A PERSONAL NODAL CYCLES STORY

When it comes to unraveling the meaning of your Nodal story, it's important to be patient with yourself, as for many of us, it's a "work in progress" story that develops over time.

Pop astrologer and author Lisa Stardust says her Lunar Nodes story has been about becoming the leader that she was born to be. Lisa was born with the South Node in Aquarius and the North Node in Leo. She is a natural-born team player who has helped and elevated the work of many people (including me). However, to truly evolve in this lifetime, what she needs to do is elevate her own career visibility. After all, anyone with the North Node in Leo is meant to shine by harnessing their creativity!

While Lisa did begin stepping into a leadership role at a corporate job, it wasn't until her second Nodal Opposition (twenty-seven to twenty-eight years old) that she began figuring out what her true passion was. At this decisive and fated moment, she realized she wanted to take her cosmic studies, which began during childhood, to a whole new professional level. Lisa had been reading charts for friends for a while, but it wasn't until this point that she was ready to announce her passion, as she had been hiding due to fear of being judged by naysayers.

Today, Lisa not only shines as a leader in the astrological and spirituality industry, she has three books and has been featured in all top media outlets worldwide.

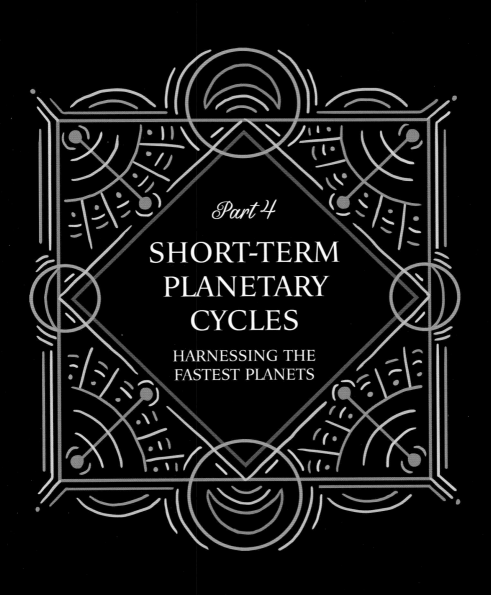

Part 4

SHORT-TERM PLANETARY CYCLES

HARNESSING THE FASTEST PLANETS

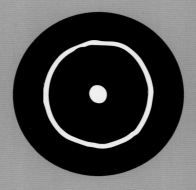

Sun

Keywords

Ego, Vitality, Life Force, Sense of Self, Creativity,
Leadership, Self-Expression, Identity, Joy, Pride,
Recognition, Confidence, Arrogance,
Personal Essence, Consciousness

Solar Archetypes

Creative Force, The King, The Yang, The Father,
The Illuminator, Male Role Model

The Astronomy of the Sun

The Sun is a star—one of a hundred billion stars just in the Milky Way galaxy. To this day, scientists have discovered that there are up to one septillion stars in the universe. The Sun is not necessarily unique, but it is special to us because our planet Earth, along with the rest of the planets and asteroids, travels around it. The Sun is the center of our solar system and revolves around another celestial body, which is called the Galactic Center.

Being a nearly perfect circular sphere of hot plasma, the Sun is 93 million miles away—but somehow, its light takes only about eight minutes to illuminate everything that it touches here on Earth. The Sun is the giver of life and "the king" star that fuels our existence.

The Astrology of the Sun

Astrologically speaking, the Sun retains its special place as the most brilliant body in our sky, as it has been venerated by all ancient cultures around the world. Much like it physically orders our solar system, the Sun is a guiding force in our birth charts that illuminates our path toward higher states of consciousness. It is "the king" of each one of our birth charts, as it represents the quality of light we came to shine to the world in this incarnation.

In your birth chart, the position of the Sun by zodiac sign, astrological house, and aspect is incredibly telling of your father or male role model. It rules your sense of identity, vitality, and the development and expression of your ego. Also known as your star sign, your Sun sign delineates your life's motivations, your sense of purpose, and how you express yourself.

Your Sun sign is your star sign, the one you've been familiar with from the moment you began reading your horoscope. Being one of the two masculine parts of yourself, the Sun in your birth chart is a guiding force that indicates your learning in this incarnation.

Embodying Sun's Higher Vibration

Regardless of which sign your Sun is in, when you are attuned to its highest vibration, you have a strong sense of self and are sure of who you are. Your solar center is attached to your solar plexus chakra, the energetic center that holds your decision-making. Being able to forge your own path without worrying about the opinions or reactions of others means you're connected with your sense of purpose, which is your Sun sign.

Since the Sun is the greatest creator of our solar system, our celestial home, when you're in tune with your Sun, you're en route to creating the life of your dreams. Even when life becomes unpredictable or intense, you always come back to your heart center, faithfully following your inner bliss.

Leadership is another word you're comfortable with when you're embodying your Sun sign—in a generous rather than ambitious way. After all, those who truly shine function as beacons of light for others to begin walking the same path of confidence and recognition.

Sun's Lower Vibration

You are under your Sun's lower vibration when you've completely lost sense of who you are or where you are going. Of course, we all have ups and downs and experience loss and deep transformation. But you know you've lost your way when you aren't able to connect with your heart and what it strives to communicate to you.

Since your Sun rules vitality and life force energy, you also know you've lost touch with it if you have fallen into sickness, have long periods of depression, or have developed an aversion to exploring your creativity. The same goes if you've fallen prey to seeing yourself only through someone else's eyes, always waiting for another person to make decisions for you.

In astrological theory, the Sun has a harder time finding its light in the signs of Libra, Aquarius, and Pisces. If you have your Sun in any of these two signs, you would benefit from taking courses in confidence, creativity, and self-expression.

Finding Your Sun Sign

Most people have read their horoscopes at least once in their life, meaning they already know their Sun sign. However, the dates provided in magazines or websites for each zodiac sign don't faithfully represent the path of the Sun, as the Sun doesn't change signs at the same time each year. In other words, if you were born "on the cusp," you might want to calculate your Sun on my website's calculator to make sure you have the correct sign.

To find your Sun sign, enter your year, month, day, and exact time of birth on this link: www.naramon.com/birth-chart-calculator. Then read the description of your Sun sign below.

Your Sun Sign, Explained

Sun in Aries
The sign of the Ram is the strongest for the Sun, making you a bold, direct, uncomplicated, and active individual. You're free-spirited, brave, and always ready for an adventure! Since you have a surplus of yang energy, it's crucial to spend it exercising and moving your body. You're focused on the here and now and might at times be too impatient for your own good. Your strong sense of self and confidence is admirable, but it should never be harnessed into competing with others.

Sun in Taurus
Being born with the Sun in Taurus gives you a smooth, steady, and grounded attitude toward life. You are attuned to the five senses and, therefore, more aware of the subtle energies of the elements. This also translates to your desire to enjoy the pleasures of life like fine food, good music, and slow living. A strong foundation is important for you to have; work hard to achieve your goals. Your weakness is an aversion to change, which you might go to great lengths to avoid.

Sun in Gemini
If you have your Sun in Gemini, you're most likely the chattiest of your group of friends. Fun, social, and approachable, you need some-one to bounce ideas off of as you're highly intellectual and easily get bored with the same old same old. You like diversity and can basically talk to anyone about anything. A serial learner, curiosity is one of your superpowers but can also be what stops you from finishing things or achieving real results.

Sun in Cancer
Being a Cancer Sun means you're a natural-born nurturer and people flock to you to receive your unconditional love and support. You're very family-oriented or a tribe kind of person. Although you take a while to

open your heart to others, once you do, you hold them in your heart and vow to protect them forever. The fact that you're emotional does not mean you're not ambitious; you're incredibly tenacious, especially when it comes to coming up with unique ways of figuring things out.

Sun in Leo
Leo is the only sign ruled by the Sun, so you're lucky if you have this combination! Confident and regal, you have an incredibly strong sense of self, owning an aura that attracts others to your orbit. Jovial, loyal, and generous, you truly have the best intentions for your people as well as the collective. Giving birth to things is one of your superpowers—you have the type of creativity that needs to be harnessed into a career or passion.

Sun in Virgo
Being born as a Virgo Sun makes you a grounded individual with a taste for all things natural and healthy. There's a healing energy to you that inspires you to achieve wholeness by aligning mind, body, and spirit. But you have another side of you that is more practical, which involves being analytical and detail-oriented. This is due to your focus and unique ability to notice what needs to be fixed, altered, organized, and refined. Any team is lucky to have you on board!

Sun in Libra
If you were born with the Sun in Libra, you're likely a social butterfly. People in general—managing, supporting, or dealing with them—is a big focus for you. One reason for this is that justice, equality, and balance are important values for you. But you're also a thinker who loves finding and weighing all the options available, as deep inside, you're an intellectual. Because you're so people-oriented, having a true sense of identity that is just yours is crucial to your long-term success.

Sun in Scorpio
If you're a Scorpio, you're a powerful being with amazing resilience and a desire to go beneath any surface. Enigmatic and mysterious, you're attracted to the unknown, the taboo, and what's behind the veil, most likely due to the need to find healing within your own life. Most

Scorpios have intense lives, as this sign craves (consciously or unconsciously) to experience the full spectrum of emotions. Never boring, your life is a fascinating journey of transformation and self-discovery!

Sun in Sagittarius

Being born under the sign of the Archer means you're fun, free-spirited, and most likely on the run! Exploration (physical or intellectual) is one of your main drives, as you enjoy being everywhere, meeting everyone, and learning about the world. You're both an optimist and an idealist, which works for you most of the time, as you're naturally lucky! Due to your desire to experience it all, the best thing you can do is have a clear goal and stick to it.

Sun in Capricorn

Ruled by Saturn, the planet of time, Capricorn is the fine wine zodiac sign that only gets better with age. This is crucial to remember in a world that prizes instant gratification. You're ambitious and have your eyes on the prize, but that does not mean you're frivolous. You know what you want, which is to build a strong legacy that stands the test of time. Behind your strong facade—as well as your great success—there's a softer interior that yearns to be expressed more.

Sun in Aquarius

Being an Aquarius means that, from an early age, you felt different. You might feel like an outcast, a rule-breaker, or even a starseed (an advanced spiritual being from another realm)—and that is what is so special about you! Something about your life involves combining tried and true methods with new and modern approaches and viewpoints. It is in this in-between where your genius lands, as part of your journey is to push humanity forward—no pressure! Freedom is one of your main values and something that must be cultivated in your career and relationships.

Sun in Pisces

If you were born with the Sun in Pisces, you're likely a mystical soul. You have this softness and magical aura about you that people feel drawn to. The chameleon-like nature you possess allows you to relate to all kinds of people and sometimes even experience their feelings. Practicing energetic protection is key for you, especially when in large crowds. A focus on creativity and inspiration is important, too, as it gives room for your rich imagination to play.

YOUR SOLAR CYCLE
One Year
Note: Your Sun probably won't be in this position within your chart. What this illustration seeks to convey is how your solar cycle works.

These are all the solar cycles you experience every single year, over the course of twelve months. While it might seem a bit difficult to understand at first, following the path of the transiting Sun—in relationship to the natal Sun in your chart—is the easiest way to begin experiencing how astrology affects you. It will also help you wrap your mind around the cyclical nature of all the bodies in our solar system.

To get even more specific dates regarding your current (or next) solar activations, head to this page: www.naramon.com/written-in-your-stars. Then match the results with the text below.

Strategies for Harnessing Your Solar Returns
Timing: Once a year, lasting for ten days
Have you ever wondered why you feel excited and refreshed during the time your birthday arrives? Besides that it is a time to embrace a spirit of celebration, the true energy behind it is that the Sun returns to the same position it is in your birth chart, from our perspective here on Earth. Below is how to harness this "trip around the Sun."

1. Take note of the themes that surface: Since this is a reset, the themes that come up in the days surrounding your birthday will remain active in your life for the next twelve months. This is what astrologers call a "solar return chart."
2. Step into the limelight: The Sun brings illumination your way now, making this a good time to act on your dreams. Whether you're applying for a job, launching your business, or giving birth to a project, the Sun can help you "be and feel seen" now.
3. Plant the seed of intention: How do you want to feel over the next year? Writing it and mentioning it out loud helps you materialize

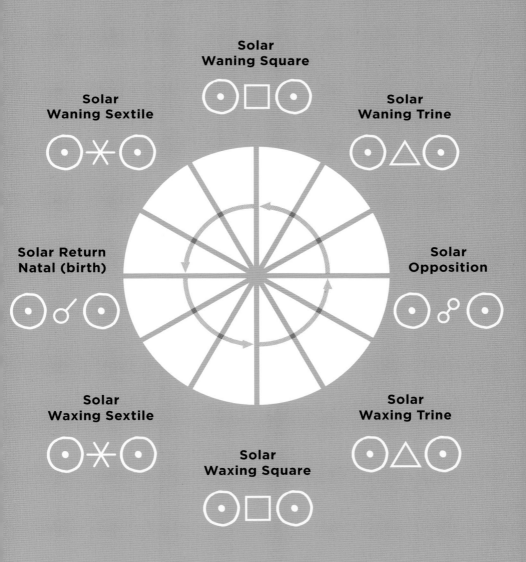

it; don't be shy about screaming it into the wind! If you can act on it, even better, as whatever you begin now will receive the Sun's impulse.

4. Be comfortable taking space: Since the Sun rules who you are and your uniqueness, this is a time to review what that means for you and show it to those around you.

Strategies for Harnessing Your Solar Sextiles
Timing: Twice a year, lasting for about six days
Happening twice a year, two months before and two months after your birthday, your Solar Sextiles can bring some of the happiest moments of the year. These are times during which the Sun's brilliance is working for you, helping you co-create with its force. And while you will most likely be feeling "in the flow" now, it helps to know when the next help from the Sun arrives so you can plan accordingly. Here are some tips:

1. Set lofty goals: You have more vitality and energy at your disposal, meaning you can accomplish more.
2. Plan activities that boost your mood: The Sun rules everything that makes you happy or brings you joy—and, therefore, these are times of enjoyment. Taking vacations, creative endeavors, and collaborations should go well at this time unless you're experiencing other intense transits. Gatherings, and being around people, should go smoothly and be fun.
3. Look out for opportunity: Those around you will be helping you out now. However, new people could also come into your orbit exactly when you need them the most, so stay aware of the signs and the opportunities that become available to you now.

Strategies for Navigating Your Solar Squares
Timing: Twice a year, lasting for ten days
Your Solar Squares are times of crisis during which challenges (small or big) tend to appear. This is a time of finding resolutions or needing to make decisions, but it is nothing you can't handle. You've been handling moments and days like these all your life. The good news is that now you know they are cyclical, so you can either expect them or prepare for them. Here are some tips:

1. Manage differences of opinions: Whether it is in your career or private life, you might run into someone wanting to move forward in a way that doesn't make sense to you. Breathe and, with patience, show the reasons behind your desired actions.
2. Control your ego: Most of the pressure now comes from other people testing either your knowledge, your abilities, or your creativity. Unless you have authority over them, they might have the winning hand, so it might be best to act on your best behavior.
3. If this is the waxing square (three months after your birthday), the challenges are directed toward something new that you are building. This is a time to get creative and look for resources or solutions in different places.
4. If this is the waning square (three months before your birthday), the pressure might be more about arriving at the finish line of important projects. If you have to redo or fix something you thought was complete, it's worth investing the time and effort to do so.

Strategies for Harnessing Your Solar Trines
Timing: Twice a year, lasting for about eight days

Harmony comes into your life now, so these are days during which things should work in your favor. The events that occur—in both career and private life—tend to go according to plan and people conspire in your favor, especially the men in your life. Here are some tips:

1. Unwind and have fun: If you're due for a vacation, these days are the perfect time to unwind and relax, as everything in your life should be balanced and flowing smoothly. Heading to a place where you can soak up the Sun's light would be quite fitting now.
2. Get ahead on your goals: If you're more in a work-hard mood now, you have the stamina and energy to not only get stuff done but to get ahead on your goals.
3. Explore creative hobbies: The Sun rules creativity in all its manifestations, so this would be a time when your juices are flowing! Take advantage of this by staying open to testing new avenues of self-expression.
4. Highlight the divine masculine in your life: Whether it's your brother, father, boyfriend, husband, or male friend, you now get the chance to spend quality time with them.

Strategies for Navigating Your Solar Oppositions
Timing: Once a year, lasting for ten days
This is the time of the year during which the Sun sits exactly across your natal Sun, activating the opposite sign. It always arrives six months after your birthday and lasts for about ten days (five days before and five days after). Oppositions require balance, as well as keeping in mind these points:

1. Focus on what truly matters: Personal projects and personal situations are likely to reach a peak at this time. Avoid spreading yourself too thin and instead focus on what is more important for you now.
2. Use your energy wisely: Since the Sun rules vitality, this can be a time of tiredness and low drive. The great news is that you can predict it so you can give yourself time to rest and the chance to avoid any activities that feel too strenuous for your body at the moment.
3. Put yourself in the other person's shoes: Someone might challenge you now (a boss, a parent, or another authority figure) and you're better off acting with care and awareness.
4. Review your life: For every action, there is a reaction—and now, the universe will show you the consequence (positive or negative) of the life you have created for yourself. Take any failures or mistakes for what they truly are: learnings.

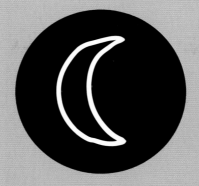

Moon

Keywords

Emotions, Nurturance, Safety, Maternal,
Instinctual, Fertility, Dreams, Subconscious
Heritage, Ancestral DNA, Memory, Moods,
Food, The Body, Survival, The Deepest Self

Lunar Archetypes

The Mother, The Queen, The Yin, Female
Role Model, The Witch, The High Priestess

The Astronomy of the Moon

Like the Sun, the Moon holds a special place in our sky. It is the Earth's only satellite and, therefore, the biggest and most brilliant object along our firmament. The Moon has been the gateway for humans to expand their understanding of the solar system. Because the Moon doesn't have an atmosphere, it has been constantly bombarded by celestial bodies such as asteroids, meteorites, and comets. As a result, the Moon and its rocky, mountainous terrain functions as a geological record of our solar system.

According to science, the Moon makes our planet more hospitable for life by moderating the Earth's movement on its axis, leading to a more stable climate. The fact that the Moon's orbit is locked into the Earth's orbit also creates the ocean's tides, which have guided humans for thousands of years. Astronomically, the Moon has a strong water connection, creating higher tides, due to water having less density than land. Samples obtained and studied between 2009 and 2018 confirmed that water exists locked inside and on the surface of the Moon in the form of ice.

The Astrology of the Moon

The astrological meaning of the Moon derives from its astronomical gifts to us. While the Sun is the most brilliant celestial body in the day sky, the Moon takes its place at night. If the Sun rules everything that is obvious and visible about our persona, the Moon rules everything that is not obvious and invisible about us—even to ourselves! If the Sun is "the king" of our birth charts, the Moon is "the queen," representing the divine feminine within.

In your birth chart, the position of the Moon by zodiac sign, astrological house, and aspect is incredibly telling of the relationship you have with your mother. It speaks of the ways you were raised, but also what your needs are in terms of feeling safe and loved. The astronomical relationship the Moon has with water makes it the astrological ruler of our feelings and our emotions. Lunar energies are so necessary to pay attention to because, since ancient times, astrologers realized the Moon is strongly connected to our bodies, ruling over what we need to feel good and whole—like sleeping, eating, resting, and being nurtured.

The Moon's Lower Vibration

The most interesting part about the Moon is that even though she rules the deeper or unseen part of ourselves, our bodies let us know if we've become disconnected from it. Some examples of this are extreme weight gain or loss, eating disorders, and at its worst, intense food allergies. Some of us experience these types of issues because we lacked nurturance at an early age, and once we become adults, it becomes our own responsibility to love ourselves by healing our inner child.

Riding the Moon's lower vibration also manifests as a disconnection with our feelings. Extreme emotional highs and lows—from hiding them one day to exaggerating them the next—is also a bypass of not truly knowing ourselves from the inside out. Luckily, with the divine feminine making a comeback in recent years, we are all rediscovering how to navigate our emotions. This also involves being in touch with the moves the Moon is performing in the sky at any given time, as following its steps guides us in understanding how the outside energies affect us at a deeper and personal level.

Embodying the Moon's Higher Vibration

When we're embodying our Moon's higher vibration, we're sensitive to the subtle energies perceived by our psyche. We notice what is below the surface, feeling our way through life with intuition rather than just what we perceive as being "real" or "logical."

Embodying lunar energies also means being comfortable in the dark, figuratively and physically. This involves listening to our bodies and having a strong connection with our gut, as the Moon rules our stomach and our eating patterns. Embodying lunar energies involves being in tune with our feelings and emotions, which, by the way, are not required to be logical or make sense!

When it comes to romantic relationships, your Moon sign will depict your day-to-day needs as well as emotional non-negotiables that should never be ignored.

Finding Your Moon Sign

Due to the Moon being the fastest-moving object in the sky, it is super important that you have an accurate time of birth to find your Moon sign. Luckily, most of us can find this by looking at our birth certificates. To find yours, enter your year, month, day, and exact time of birth on this link: www.naramon.com/birth-chart-calculator. Then read the description of your Moon sign below.

Your Moon Sign, Explained

Moon in Aries

If your Moon is in Aries, you need action and movement—especially during difficult days and moments. A steady and vigorous workout routine is your way of navigating your emotional landscape. For you, the forty-eight-hour rule is a must to follow, as you tend to get riled up quite quickly. Wait forty-eight hours before acting impulsively. Luckily, it's just as easy for you to forgive and forget. Passionate and excitable, you need adventure, and those who are brave enough to get on your boat are in for a fun ride!

Moon in Taurus

Congratulations! Taurus is the Moon's absolute favorite sign to be, which gives you a grounded emotional demeanor. Others flock to you whenever in need of support, as you're devoted to the people you care about. Attracting and creating wealth is one of your gifts. You are a creature of habit and need a certain amount of comfort in life, as you're all about living "the good life." Embracing change is something to work on, as you tend to linger in situations longer than you should.

Moon in Gemini

If your Moon is in chatty Gemini, you approach emotions through an intellectual lens. This creates a nonstop loop of conversations about your inner workings but might also prevent you from actually feeling them. When you bring your attention from your mind to your heart, remember that emotions aren't logical. You need communication to feel nurtured. Practices like free-flow writing can really help you attune to both your feelings as well as intuition.

Moon in Cancer

Congratulations, moonchild! Cancer is a very comfortable sign for the Moon, which gives you a deep inner life. You're emotionally resilient and tenacious in the defense of the one you love. Feeling safe is a priority for you and the reason why you might take a little time to open up to others. Once you open up, your nurturing warmth is unmatchable and the reason why so many flock to you for advice. Whenever feeling moody, you need space to be alone and in your feels.

Moon in Leo

Being born with the Moon in Leo makes you a charismatic, optimistic, and sunny individual. You're generous and expect the same in return from the ones you love. Those around you feel attracted to your light and fun demeanor, as you bring energy and fire to any situation. This, of course, can sometimes turn into dramatic situations and scenarios— after all, life is never boring with you! Creativity in all its forms is one of your superpowers and the way to cope when life gets intense.

Moon in Virgo

Having the Moon in Virgo gives you a cerebral approach to emotions, giving you the desire to compartmentalize and analyze feelings. You can gain a lot by allowing yourself to just sit with your emotions, accepting them for what they are. Those around you love that you're incredibly thoughtful, as being helpful is something that truly makes you happy. Being of service to society is something that is ingrained in your emotional nature and something that could even become a career or life path.

Moon in Libra

If your Moon is in Libra, you were gifted a soft and polite demeanor when it comes to your emotional makeup. Creating harmony and balance within your life and relationships is a priority, as is for things to be fair. While you do tend to have an intellectual approach to feelings, your desire to avoid conflict at all costs helps you arrive at win-win scenarios. In the end, you are a people person who understands that relationships take time, effort, and understanding.

Moon in Scorpio

Being born with the Moon in Scorpio means you have an intense emotional life, as you feel everything very deeply. Your no-nonsense approach to life means you're adverse to superficiality, especially to people who are too scared of exploring life's deepest mysteries. When you get involved in relationships, you give all your heart and expect the same in return. However, leaving connections that no longer light you up inside might be a struggle and something you're always invited to evolve out of.

Moon in Sagittarius

Having your Moon in the sign of the Archer gives you a rich emotional life. You feel at your best when you're exploring, learning, connecting, and absorbing knowledge. A tribe type of person, you attract people who, like you, approach life with optimism and gusto! The forty-eight-hour rule is crucial to pay attention to, as you tend to get overly excited about things—only to change your mind the next day. When it comes to expressing yourself, you're very direct, sometimes to the point of being blunt.

Moon in Capricorn

If your Moon is in Capricorn, you are one driven individual! You understand the concept of long-term gain and are fearless in putting in the effort to build the life of your dreams. After all, you were raised by successful and ambitious parents who taught you the value of showing up for yourself and others. Expressing emotions and learning to show your vulnerable side is not your forte and is something you must strive to learn when it comes to having thriving relationships.

Moon in Aquarius

Having your Moon placed in Aquarius means you're emotionally invested in making the world a better place. As a maverick and trend-setter, part of your mission is to bring a more modern approach to the world of relationships. After all, you need the freedom to experience all that life has to offer, which includes friendship and romance. While pushing the boundaries is one of your gifts, it's crucial to remember that not everyone experiences feelings through such an intellectual lens.

Moon in Pisces

Having the Moon in Pisces gives you a soft and soulful demeanor. Highly idealistic and romantic, you're all about expressing what's lurking beneath your magical surface. You have a dreamy and captivating aura that brings comfort to those around you, as you're a soul-tribe type of person. Fully merging your feelings with those of others is what feels most natural to you—however, this can also bring confusion when a more pragmatic approach is needed within a relationship. While boundaries aren't always fun, they are required to create successful connections.

YOUR LUNAR CYCLE
One Month (29 days)

Note: Your Moon probably won't be in this position within your chart. What this illustration seeks to convey is how your lunation cycle works.

On page 156 are all the lunar cycles you experience each month over the course of roughly four weeks, since the lunar cycle spans twenty-nine-and-a-half days. The reason why is that the Moon is the fastest-moving body in our sky, always changing and shifting. Lunar movements are fast and the reason why the energies change so much from one day to the next!

To get even more specific dates regarding your current (or next) Lunar activations, head to this page: www.naramon.com/written-in-your-stars. Then match the results with the text below.

Strategies for Harnessing Your Lunar Returns

Timing: Once a month, lasting for a day

Your Lunar Return, when the traveling Moon goes back to the exact same place in the sky it was when you were born, is the most important part of your monthly lunar cycle. It is a reinvigoration of your inner world, reminding you of the things that are more important to you. And while your Lunar Return is short, it is one of the most important days of the month. Here are some tips:

1. Take this day as an inception moment: Due to the planets always moving in the sky, every Lunar Return is different.

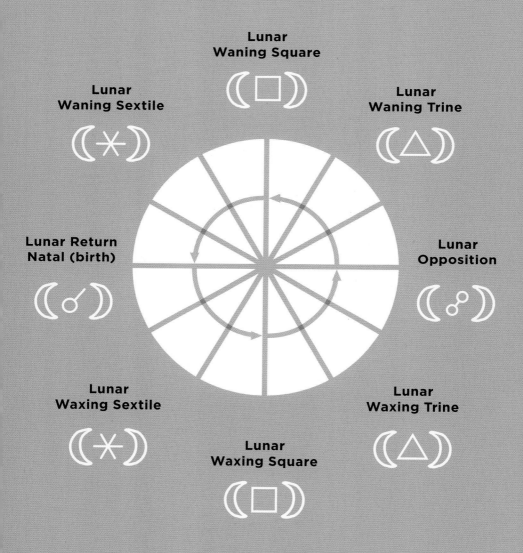

On this special day, you will notice new themes—and more than anything, feelings—coming up. Notice and take note of them, as they could stay active for the next twenty-nine days, until your next Lunar Return.

2. Seek emotional release: If there was ever a time to give yourself the time, space, and privacy to be in your feels, that time is now! This is also an opportunity to go down memory lane and reflect on some of your life's sweetest moments.

3. Rest or at least sleep in: The Moon rules sleeping and comfort, so it's normal to need more of that. However, if your Moon is in a fire sign (Aries, Leo, and Sagittarius), you might feel more energetic than tired.

4. Attune to your feminine side: Women in your life might become important around now (your mom, sister, or girlfriends). Pay attention to the vibes they're bringing to your orbit, most likely teaching you something.

Strategies for Harnessing Your Lunar Sextiles
Timing: Twice a month, lasting for about a day
The sextile is an aspect of opportunity, but you are bound to miss it if you're not paying attention to the possibilities right in front of you. Here are some tips for how to make the best of this sweet day:

1. Spend time with family: We each have a very specific relationship with family, but regardless of it, these days could bring easiness when interacting with our clan. This would also be a good time for presentations and being around big crowds of people, as you're bound to feel comfortable in your own skin.

2. Explore your spirituality: Since the Moon is instinctual, you might notice the subtle energies around you more now. This is a good time to meditate, do rituals, or explore the richness of mystical arts.

3. Trust your instincts: The Moon is giving you powerful vision now, so whatever you sense when spending time with others should be correct. Following your hunches now helps you create rapport with others.

4. Respond to the need for intimacy: Because you feel good in your own skin, you're more inclined to connect at a deeper level. This is a fabulous time for a date night, spending time with your VIPs, or making new friends.

Strategies for Navigating Your Lunar Squares
Timing: Twice a month, lasting for about a day
Depending on how emotional you are, your Lunar Squares can be a time of crisis. Sometimes, it's a reaction to an event; other times, you just feel moody! This will be especially true if you, like me, were born on a Quarter Moon phase. Here are some tips on how to handle these two emotional days:

1. Avoid reacting: Your emotional nature is heightened now, making you a bit more susceptible to other people's energies. If someone pushes your buttons, consider leaving the conversation for another time.
2. Avoid large gatherings: If possible, avoid planning any big meetings or events during these two days, as people might get on your nerves. Truthfully, it's you and not them, so act accordingly.
3. Practice emotional discernment: These are not days of emotional clarity—but the complete opposite of that. Before acting impulsively, sleep on it. This is especially true for you if your Moon is in a fire sign—Aries, Leo, or Sagittarius.
4. Notice tensions surfacing: If you're wondering if there is tension between you and someone, it will become obvious now. But remember, it's a time to notice but not act on what you perceive.

Strategies for Harnessing Your Lunar Trines
Timing: Twice a month, lasting for about a day
In astrology, the trine is the most positive aspect, making these days emotionally flowy and self-nurturing. Knowing when they come around helps you plan accordingly, especially if you're really in tune with your Moon sign. Here are some tips:

1. Recharge your batteries: Rest and relaxation are appealing to you now, bringing a good time to go pamper yourself, take care of your body, and go to bed early to catch up on sleep or rest.

2. Connect deeper: These are days when you might want to share more of yourself or explore relationship-related conversations, as others will be in tune with what you're feeling.
3. Nurture who or what you care for: Your maternal instincts are activated, bringing the perfect time to connect with your children, plants, pets, or whatever you enjoy loving and nurturing.
4. Host gatherings: Since the Moon relates to our home, these are times during which you might feel in the mood to host friends, dinner parties, or gatherings. The same goes for attending big gatherings or events.

Strategies for Navigating Your Lunar Oppositions
Timing: Once a month, lasting for a day
Your Lunar Opposition, when the traveling Moon momentarily sits exactly across your natal Moon, is the second-most important part of your monthly lunar cycle. Oppositions bring the need for balance and, in this case, this is a time to be—or at least try to be, emotionally even-keeled. Your Lunar Oppositions will be more impactful if your Moon is in a water sign (Cancer, Scorpio, or Pisces). Here are some tips:

1. Expect to be moody: Today might be one of those days you get up on the wrong side of the bed. Taking the time to give your body what it needs now could be a game-changer, so focus on that.
2. Seek emotional balance: Someone's feelings might oppose yours now. Instead of playing the blame game, it might be best to try to see the other person's position. Remember, feelings don't need to make sense, so instead of trying to box them, agree to disagree concerning how you *feel*.
3. Embody emotional detachment: If dealing with a group, you might feel like the collective vibe doesn't get you. Your feelings are powerful now and are most likely being intensified.
4. Seek peace and harmony in your relationships: If you're not naturally an emotional person (if your Moon is in Virgo, Capricorn, or Aquarius), this could be very noticeable to those around you. Showing that you care is now a gateway to finding a deeper flow.

Mercury

Keywords

Mind, Intellect, Communication, Writing, Speech,
Listening, Thought Process, Information, Memory,
Messages, Knowledge, Wit, Learning,
Eloquence, Perception

Mercury Archetypes

The Messenger, The Trickster, The Author,
The Speaker, The Shapeshifter,
The Magician

The Astronomy of Mercury

Mercury is the smallest planet in our solar system, but its place in it as the planet closest to the Sun makes it incredibly important, as well as mysterious and ghostly. Unlike the other "inner planets" closest to Earth (Venus, Mars, Jupiter, and Saturn), Mercury is hard to see, as it is always following the Sun. Mercury can only be spotted either at sunrise or at sunset—and that is only when it separates enough from the Sun, from our perspective here on Earth. Mercury lacks an atmosphere, meaning that its temperatures fluctuate extremely, going from very hot to very cold and vice versa.

But what makes Mercury an astronomical anomaly is its speed; Mercury performs a full loop around the Sun in just eighty-eight days. This is the reason why Mercury goes retrograde so often: three to four times a year, spending thirty to forty percent of its time in retrograde motion.

It's important to mention that retrograde motion is "apparent"—it's an optical illusion, created by the difference in speed between Mercury and the Earth as they both travel around the Sun. The effect is similar to passing a slower car in another lane while driving, where the slower car may appear to be moving backward.

The Astrology of Mercury

Mercury's astrological meaning derives from its strategic place in relationship to the star it tours around and around without end. Since the Sun represents who you are and your "sense of self," Mercury represents your mind and your intellect. In other words, you can't *be* without the possibility of *thinking* and *reasoning*.

Everything that Mercury rules—thoughts, communication, memory, and perception—is vital to our ability to exist and interact with our environment. Whenever you're reading a text, writing an email, having a meeting, talking with a friend, listening to music, or giving a presentation, you are in the realm of Mercury. How Mercury is placed in your birth chart illustrates your intellect, how you talk, your ability to listen, and how you process information.

Mercury's mysterious and ghostly appearances in our sky represent the puzzling workings of the mind, always changing and ever-evolving. While we sometimes dread this trickster's retrogrades, we can also thank them for the opportunity to reset and revitalize our perception, allowing us to see the same thing from a different perspective.

Embodying Mercury's Higher Vibration

Known as Hermes in Greek mythology, Mercury has been the "messenger of the gods" since ancient times. You are embodying Mercury's higher vibration when you're expressing yourself in any type of way or form. This process starts in the mind as an idea, passes through your mouth (speech) or your hands (writing), and culminates when it becomes a material result. Examples include a book, a song, or even just a presentation or a social media post. You and I are doing a Mercurial thing here: I wrote a book and you are learning from it, and we are both embodying Mercury's higher vibration. We are learning, teaching, and exchanging ideas in the spirit of absorbing knowledge, which requires sustaining a true curiosity of the mind.

Mercury's Lower Vibration

Mercury—the fastest-moving planet and the one that goes retrograde the most—is naturally shifty. Mercury is the ultimate shapeshifter, continually adapting to the energies around it while staying neutral. Symbolically, this means that the mind is designed to do the same: shift, morph, and adapt.

You are embodying the lower vibration of Mercury when you get overly attached to your mind processes and ways of thinking. Phrases like "that doesn't make sense to me," "that's not the way I think," or "I disagree with . . . " occur way too often. And while they follow our belief system, they can easily prevent us from absorbing the type of information and knowledge that could transform us.

As mentioned earlier in this chapter, the astronomical fact that planet Mercury (thinking) travels so close to the Sun (sense of self) easily leads to the misunderstanding that we *are* our thoughts—that if we change them, we lose a part of ourselves. When you truly realize that you are not your thoughts, you open yourself to a whole new world of possibilities.

Finding Your Mercury Sign

Finding your Mercury sign is relatively easy and can even be easily guessed before adding your birth data to a calculator. Since Mercury is always following the Sun, it can only be as far as one sign before or one sign after your Sun sign. For example, if you are a Scorpio Sun, your Mercury sign can only be in three signs: Libra, Scorpio, or Sagittarius. If you are a Taurus Sun, your Mercury sign will either be in Aries, Taurus, or Gemini, and so on.

To get your Mercury sign, add your birth date (day, month, year, and time) to this calculator: www.naramon.com/birth-chart-calculator. Then read your style of processing information by reading your Mercury sign below.

Your Mercury Sign, Explained

Mercury in Aries
Speaking, writing, information-processing, and decision-making—you do it all fast as you're not messing around! Sometimes, you might even feel like your mouth can't catch up with your mind, or that conversations drag for too long for your taste. While this energetic approach to thought processing elevates you whenever promoting your ideas, it can also make you miss important details in the process. Try to become aware of how others may perceive your direct approach as impatience or anger.

Mercury in Taurus
People might think that you are indecisive—but you aren't, you are just methodical and need to take your time before arriving at a decision. The great news is that the patience you ask from others you're also giving in return, as you don't mind waiting to get to the most optimal option. This is because once you've made up your mind, good luck to anyone who might try to make you change it! You may be stubborn, but when you say you're going to do something, you come through.

Mercury in Gemini
If you have Mercury in Gemini, you're likely a master of communications. Logical and intellectual, you probably have a word-focused career, as you love to talk, listen, and exchange ideas and information. Your mind gets bored easily and needs constant stimulation, which is great for learning as long as you can keep your focus on the subject at hand. The truth is that being mentally scattered might be a problem for you; this shouldn't be confused with multitasking.

Mercury in Cancer

If you have Mercury in Cancer, your communication style is careful and nurturing. Since words carry an emotional tone for you more than for others, you choose yours wisely. You absorb information via your emotions and find it easy to align your mind with your heart—but it's important to remember that not everyone has this same filter. Since you get to know people by feeling their words, when you're not comfortable around someone, you shut down, finding it hard to open up to them.

Mercury in Leo

Your communication style is loud, proud, and regal! As soon as you begin talking, your words command attention, as they illuminate that which others haven't yet noticed. An excellent idea promoter, you excel at entertaining folks with your fun dialogue, getting your message across. The problem comes when someone disagrees with you, as one of the hardest things to do is to get you to change your mind. Practicing objectivity during these times is your key to success.

Mercury in Virgo

Having Mercury in Virgo gives you a special talent for the written word, as this is the winning combination many writers and editors own. You love to express yourself but prefer to do it in a more sophisticated way than just loudly expressing your opinions. As a masterful analyst, you notice all the details that others miss, overlook, or completely get wrong. You're an invaluable member of the teams you belong to, as it's rare to find your sense of practicality combined with such a hard work ethic.

Mercury in Libra

If you have Mercury in Libra, you struggle with decision-making due to your deep desire to arrive at a fair and just conclusion. You're a perfectionist when it comes to setting the tone for everyone to have their say and express their opinion. And if you disagree with them, you certainly have the intellectual skills to let them know they're wrong while getting them to smile back at you! After all, your charming eloquence helps you get away with what few people can.

Mercury in Scorpio

Having Mercury in Scorpio gives you an X-ray–like ability to read between the lines and see the true message behind speech. It might not even be about the subject—at least not as much as the mystery. You own the mind of a detective! One of your natural gifts is your ability to deeply focus on the task at hand, but if you're not careful, this gift can quickly give way to obsession. After all, your thought process is instinctual and intuitive, never failing when it comes to getting to the bottom of things.

Mercury in Sagittarius

You are an optimistic thinker with a philosophical streak that brings a sense of freshness to every meeting and conversation. While noticing the details might not be your forte, seeing the big picture is, as your innate gift is to open doors to new possibilities. You are a tireless optimist, which can work for or against you, depending on how grounded and focused you are. Having your mind focused on one thing at a time is your avenue to find success, as is constantly absorbing knowledge.

Mercury in Capricorn

Having Mercury in Capricorn means you are an industrious individual with an incredible ability to think (and plan) long-term. You understand how time works, as your thought process is methodical, pragmatic, and grounded. Some might say you're a bit serious—but what they're tapping into is your choosiness with words. For you, less is more, preferring to have meaningful rather than more conversations. When people throw a bunch of ideas out, you first compartmentalize them to better understand them. Your mind works linearly.

Mercury in Aquarius

Having Mercury in Aquarius means your thought process holds a contradiction—it's pragmatic but at the same time unconventional. You're endlessly curious, always wondering, pondering, and posing the types of questions that would never cross anyone else's mind. A wise intellectual, you're always ready for exciting and long debates that, most of the time, you end up winning. It's not that you can't be objective—that's one of your superpowers—but in the end, you always stick with the most "logical" choice or explanation, regardless of the nature of the discussion.

**Mercury
Waning Square**

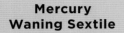

**Mercury
Waning Sextile**

**Mercury
Waning Trine**

**Mercury
Return Natal
(birth)**

**Mercury
Opposition**

**Mercury
Waxing Sextile**

**Mercury
Waxing Square**

**Mercury
Waxing Trine**

Mercury in Pisces

If you have Mercury in Pisces, your thinking process involves your feelings. This means that there's nothing linear about making decisions or arriving at conclusions, which of course, involves making room to change your mind. When you talk, it's as if you are reciting a poem, slowly creating the atmosphere for the idea that you're trying to convey. In your ideal world, there's no room for harsh words, so when they happen, you have no other option than drifting off to fantasyland.

YOUR MERCURY CYCLE
One Year

Note: Your Mercury probably won't be in this position within your chart. What this illustration seeks to convey is how your Mercury cycle works. However, it does not include retrogrades, as each retrograde of Mercury is unique, bringing a different flavor each time.

At left are all the Mercury-Mercury activations you experience every single year, over twelve months. Unlike the Sun cycles, Mercury's are less predictable due to retrogrades of Mercury. While most of the Mercury activations you experience will happen once a year for about eight days, if Mercury goes retrograde while performing an activation with your natal Mercury, the same activation could happen twice or three times, with one of them lasting for up to eighteen days.

To get even more specific dates regarding your current (or next) Mercury activations, head to this page: www.naramon.com/written-in-your-stars, then match the results with the text below.

Strategies for Harnessing Your Mercury Returns

Timing: Once a year. (If Mercury goes retrograde in your Mercury sign, it could happen two to three times within that year.)

Happening very close to your birthday, your Mercury Return is a time when communication accelerates. Your mind experiences a reinvigoration of its natural thinking process, bringing busyness but also the ideal time to intellectually self-inspect yourself. Here are some tips:

1. Study your slower planetary cycles: Since Mercury is the "cosmic messenger," when it returns to the exact place it was when you were born, it will serve as a trigger for the rest of the planetary cycles

you're currently experiencing. For example, if you're currently experiencing your Saturn Return (twenty-nine to thirty years old) or your Uranus Opposition (early forties), it will bring information concerning your handling of this bigger, more meaningful return.

2. Schedule important meetings: Unless Mercury is retrograde, your mind will be sharp and receptive, giving you articulation and the gift of gab. Since you're feeling more objective and detached than normal, this is the time for important business meetings or difficult personal conversations.

3. Follow your curiosity: Your hunger for knowledge is activated now, and if you follow it by enrolling in a course or master class, your learning could be very successful.

4. Stay focused: You will now feel Mercury's butterfly nature—and while it might be fun jumping from one conversation to the next, doing so might spread your efforts thin. By focusing your elevated mental agility on one goal, you can get a lot done.

5. Plan a trip or go travel: Mercury rules short-distance travel, creating the ideal vibe for a road trip or weekend getaway. If Mercury is retrograde, make sure to check your car before heading out, however!

Strategies for Harnessing Your Mercury Sextiles

Timing: Two to four times a year (depending on Mercury's retrograde cycle), lasting for about five days.

The sextile is an aspect of opportunity, meaning that you have a window of chance when all things Mercury (thinking, writing, and research) work in your favor. Here are some tips:

1. Work on difficult tasks: A puzzling project that requires precision or tedious attention to detail could truly benefit from your ability to examine it from every possible angle. This is especially true if you're currently experiencing a Neptune activation (see the Neptune chapter).

2. Keep the lines of communication open: If you've been hunting for a piece of information, it might come via a text, email, call, or an aha moment. Even a subtle sign could be a game-changer now, so watch for one.

3. Organize your life: You have clarity of mind, especially with numbers and detailed work—take advantage of this by creating an Excel sheet of your finances, updating your resume, or doing any type of business analysis.

4. Sign papers: Unless Mercury is retrograde now, you have an eagle-like ability to understand the fine print, making this an opportune time to sign contracts, write papers, take exams, and negotiate agreements. If Mercury is retrograde while you experience this sextile, try leaving room for negotiations in your contract. Because the sextile is an opportune aspect, the negotiations will most likely work in your favor.

Strategies for Navigating Your Mercury Squares

Timing: Two times a year, lasting for about five days. (If Mercury goes retrograde in your Mercury sign, one of these could multiply to three times.)

The square is an aspect of crisis, but with the right attitude, it can be incredibly helpful, especially in the long term. Revisit the section "Mercury's Lower Vibration" to get an idea of how it works. Here are some tips:

1. Adjust your thinking: This is when the universe will test your ability to expand your mental boundaries, and if you resist it, it could bring clashes with others. If you don't see room for agreement, it's best to delay any negotiations or decision-making.

2. Be flexible: You will receive a lot of emails, texts, and phone calls that you will have to react to by making a decision or giving an opinion. You will most likely get pushback, and the more adaptable you stay, the better the outcome will be.

3. Avoid scattering your energy: Since life gets busy now, you could end up wasting a lot of time on things that do not matter. If you have deadlines or important work to do, try leaving less important conversations or meetings for another time.

4. Take breaks: The type of work that normally does not drain you could do so. To avoid mental burnout, take time for naps, walks, or other breaks.

Strategies for Harnessing Your Mercury Trines

Timing: Two times a year, lasting for about five days. (If Mercury goes retrograde in your Mercury sign, one of these could multiply to three times)

As Mercury travels in the sky, it is forming a positive aspect with your natal Mercury. This means that mental energies are working in your favor, giving you a window of positive interactions with the outside world. Here are some tips for making the best of this bi-yearly activation:

1. Design your own mantras: The mantra "your thoughts create your reality" takes flight now, bringing the perfect time to sit down to create the mantras that will help you manifest your dream life.
2. Stay alert for synchronicity: Helpful information comes now in the form of dreams, messages, signs, and even what would seem to be just an ordinary coincidence.
3. Send requests or applications: This is a positive time to apply for jobs, send pitches, or ask to collaborate with someone. The chance of you getting a "yes" increases at this time.
4. Focus on business or commercial transactions: Since Mercury rules commerce, this is a good time for planning or even putting in place a new business strategy. You're mentally agile and should be able to come up with lucrative ideas.

Strategies for Navigating Your Mercury Oppositions

Timing: Once a year, lasting for about five days. (If Mercury goes retrograde in your Mercury sign, one of these could multiply to three times)

The opposition is an aspect of tension that requires balance. Most likely, you will find this tension in the outer world, during conversations and meetings, as others will be mirroring back at you what your current learnings are. Here are some tips:

1. Receive feedback: This is the time when others (bosses, co-workers, friends) will have opinions opposite yours, and their input can bring you a much more whole way of viewing things.

2. Zero in on your timeline: You are relatively halfway through your Solar Return (birthday), bringing a great time to look back at what you have accomplished, since then so you can figure out what has worked and what hasn't, and make the necessary changes over the next six months.

3. Avoid impulsive decision-making: Your mind is getting challenged now, creating rushed thinking and nervousness. If you are feeling these effects, it means that making an important decision could backfire or bring negative consequences. Since this is a quick transit (unless Mercury is retrograde), it's best to postpone closing on deals.

4. Act with awareness: Without knowing it, you might now be going through the motions without giving important things a second thought. Move slowly and with care.

Venus

Keywords

Pleasure, Love, Beauty, Art, Aesthetic Taste,
Relationships, Harmony, Sensuality, Money and
Finances, Enjoyment, Self-Worth, Attraction,
Vanity, Likes and Dislikes

Venus Archetypes

The Lover, The Artist, The Diplomat,
The Aesthetician, The Femme Fatale,
The Whore, Divine Feminine Archetype

The Astronomy of Venus

Due to its reflective cloud composition, Venus is the brightest planet in our solar system, often perceived as a twinkly star in our firmament. Being the second planet from the Sun, Venus is also the hottest, reaching scorching high temperatures due to its massive and dense atmosphere.

Similar to Mercury, Venus is always following the Sun from our perspective here on Earth, taking a total of 224.7 days to perform a full circle around our star. However, when studying this planet's movements closer, astronomers have noticed an overall cycle that adds up to eight years, which includes the two conjunctions (alignments) that Venus forms with the Sun, within that period. As shown below, this entire cycle draws an imaginary five-pointed star (pentagram) that endlessly loops around Earth, beautifully repeating itself again and again.

The Astrology of Venus

The depth of meaning Venus has in our lives derives from its closeness and unique and artistic dance with both the Sun and Earth. Since in astrology, the Sun represents "who we are" or our "unique essence," Venus represents something just as important when it comes to identity: how we relate to others.

Venus' beauty and scorching hot temperatures could not be more representative of how we humans experience the full spectrum of relating to one another. Astrologically, Venus rules pleasure, love, relationships, and money. Venus themes are and feel extremely personal, as how we handle them bring us moments of everything from divine joy and pure ecstasy to sadness and major heartbreak.

Its bright appearance in the sky as well as the flower petals Venus forms around our planet are the reasons why Venus also rules beauty, harmony, and artistic taste. In your birth chart, Venus speaks of your personal values and your love style. It denotes your sense of style, how you experience pleasure, what you like (and dislike)—and most importantly, how you attract what your heart desires.

Lastly, the relationship of Venus with the Sun within your chart will speak of how you handle relationships and matters of the heart.

The first illustration shows the eight-year cycle of Venus without the planets being shown. The second illustration shows the same cycle with the planets being present: the blue dot is Earth, the orange dot is the Sun, and the pink dot is Venus.

Morning Star Venus

If you were born with Venus as a morning star (when it is ahead of the Sun in the zodiac wheel):

- You are ambitious when it comes to attracting what you want—whether that is a job, friends, or romantic partners.
- You might be more sexual than sensual as this is Venus' ying (more masculine expression) side.
- When it comes to love, you're more spontaneous, free-spirited, and trusting of others—sometimes to your detriment.
- You tend to sacrifice yourself to help or elevate others.

Dark Venus (Venus Combust)

If you were born with Venus within eight degrees from the Sun:

- For you, this lifetime is about big lessons in love, pleasure, and self-worth.
- Your desire for romance or attention might burn you at times.
- Your relationships might tend to go up or down, perhaps full of dramatic moments.
- You're highly artistic and refined, especially if both your Venus and Sun are in Taurus, Capricorn, Aquarius, or Pisces.
- **Exception:** If Venus is in the same exact degree (within 17 minutes) as your Sun, you have Venus Cazimi, which gives you access to success and perhaps even an elevated social status.

Evening Star Venus
If you were born with Venus as an evening star (when it is after the Sun in the zodiac wheel):

- You're connected to this planet's goddess mythological expression, the Greek Aphrodite, making you highly feminine and sensual.
- It's easier for you to attract all things Venus: love, pleasure, money, and luxury.
- You have a strong sense of style and aesthetics.
- You put yourself before others.

Venus' Lower Vibration
Venus is considered a "benefic" planet, meaning that its nature is mainly positive. However, the fact that Venus rules relationships of all kinds (romantic as well as friendships) means that things can get messy in that department.

You are embodying your Venus' lower vibration when this part of your life is either too turbulent or missing. The range would go from being afraid to seek heartfelt connections to drowning in an unhealthy romantic pattern, repeating the same story with different people. At some point along our journey, we have all experienced romantic obsessions, sexual fixations, and even cheating scandals. If one of those rings true to you, you've experienced the dark side of lover Venus!

Another way that Venus' lower vibration manifests is a disconnection with the feminine side. Due to patriarchy approaching its end of life, this is luckily changing—but for many centuries, men, in particular, have been judged whenever showing their more vulnerable and receptive side, which relates to Venus.

Embodying Venus' Higher Vibration
Since Venus rules all the things that make your heart sing—and, therefore, your powers of attraction and manifestation—it's a planet to constantly feed. Contrary to what you might think, this is especially true when life gets tough! You are embodying your Venus when you're seeking and leaving room to truly experience that which pleases you and makes you happy. You prioritize the things, vibes, and practices that make you feel good and connected to your essence. This also involves

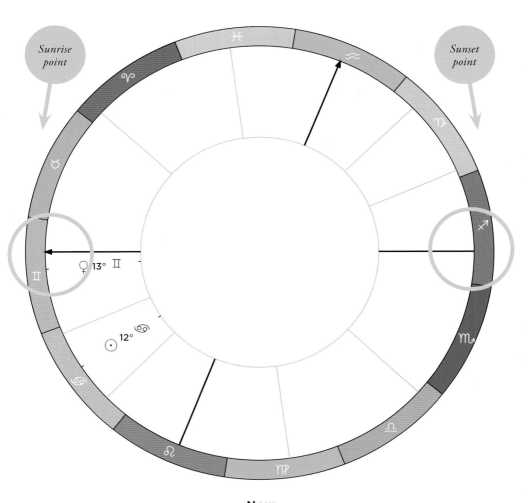

Sunrise point

Sunset point

♀ 13° ♊

☉ 12° ♋

Now
Jul 04, 2022
3:35:59 AM PDT
Lat 37° N 48' 17.0"
Lng 122° W 16' 21.0"
Placidus
Tropical
Geocentric

Example of a birth chart with Venus as a morning star

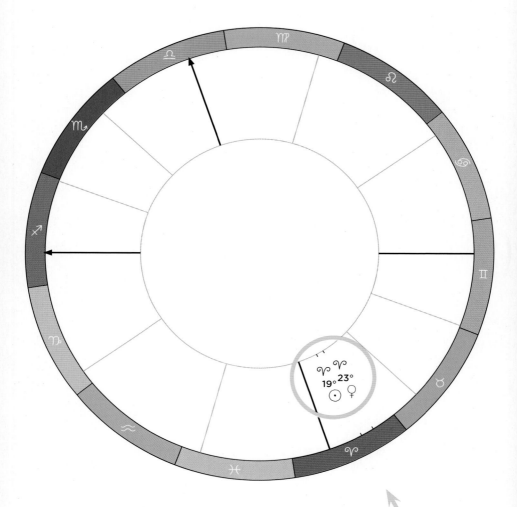

Now
Apr 09, 2021
2:35:59 AM PDT
Lat 37° N 48' 17.0"
Lng 122° W 16' 21.0"
Placidus
Tropical
Geocentric

Example of a birth chart with Venus combust

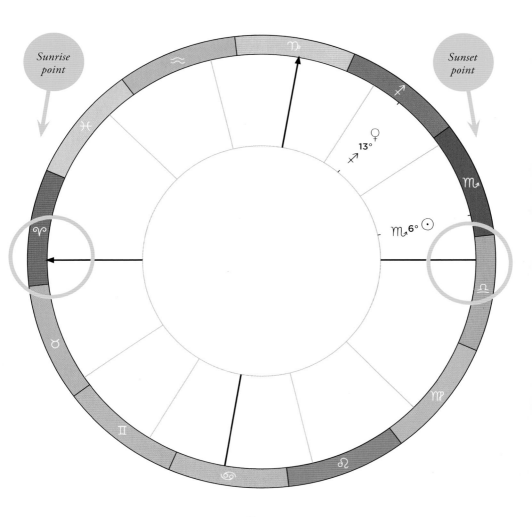

Now
Oct 28, 2024
5:35:59 AM PDT
Lat 37° N 48' 17.0"
Lng 122° W 16' 21.0"
Placidus
Tropical
Geocentric

Sunrise point

Sunset point

Example of a birth chart with Venus as an evening star

being very clear about what (or who) you do not want to be around, as Venus rules your taste but also what you dislike.

This will, of course, depend a lot on your Venus sign. For example, if you have Venus in Aries, you most likely seek action and hate boredom. If your Venus is in Sagittarius, it's crucial to travel or mentally explore new subjects, especially when you're hoping to run into some inspiration.

Finding Your Venus Sign

Like finding your Mercury sign, finding your Venus sign is relatively easy. Since Venus is always following the Sun, it can only be as far as two signs before or two signs after your Sun sign. For example, if you are a Leo Sun, your Venus sign can only be in Gemini, Cancer, Leo, Virgo, or Libra. Similarly, if you are a Capricorn Sun, your Venus can only be in Scorpio, Sagittarius, Capricorn, Aquarius, or Pisces.

To get your Venus sign, add your birth date (day, month, year, and time) to this calculator: www.naramon.com/birth-chart-calculator. Then read how you approach pleasure, love, relationships, and money in the next section.

Your Venus Sign, Explained

Venus in Aries

You are quick and direct when it comes to matters of the heart! When you want something (or someone), you're not one to wait—you're quick to go after your heart's desires. This is refreshing and charming, but you must be careful that, when it comes to love, you're actually into the person and not just the thrill of the chase. The truth is that you need fun and action in your life, and not everyone can keep up with your on-the-go demeanor.

Venus in Taurus

Taurus is one of the strongest signs for Venus, making you a grounded type of person who truly appreciates the pleasures of slow living. You require a certain amount of comfort—and luckily, it's easy for you to attract wealth to have such a lifestyle. This easiness to attract what you wish translates into your romantic life—but that does not mean you jump into relationships fast. Quite the opposite; you take a while to seal the deal, as once committed, you're in it for the long haul.

Venus in Gemini

You see love and approach relationships through an intellectual lens. More than being attracted to someone's physical traits, you fall enamored of their eloquence and intelligence. And more likely than not, the feeling is mutual. You need constant mental stimulation, and if you don't receive it, you have no problem seeking it somewhere else. After all, your romantic makeup is the epitome of a butterfly jumping from one flower to the next, finding bliss in the mantra: "Variety is the spice of life."

Venus in Cancer

If you have this planet-sign combination, you're likely a sensitive soul. Regardless of your gender, you are in touch with your feminine side, which is the reason why others feel at ease when around you. Romantically, you're traditional and not one to take risks; you prefer having a true sense of security and knowing where you stand. When it comes to money, you're somewhat frugal, preferring to spend it on creating a comfortable abode and making happy the ones you love.

Venus in Leo

Daring and passionate, you're that shinny luminary that people orbit around, as life is never boring when you're around. You have a warm aura that magnetizes friends, lovers, wealth—and especially . . . attention! Dramatic displays are your specialty, but they can also be your underdoing. Showing generosity to those around you makes you happy, but you also expect the same in return, especially from your romantic partners. Sticking to your promises and commitments comes naturally, but if you're not getting what you need, you will eventually move on and find it.

Venus in Virgo

This planet-sign combination gives you a pragmatic streak when it comes to matters of love, friendship, and money. For you, less is more, preferring classy instead of dramatic or bold displays of affection. You show devotion by listening, helping, and showing up for those you love exactly when they need you the most. You're highly cerebral, analytical, and productive, but paying the same attention to your body and sense of wellness helps you find wholeness and comfort in your own skin.

Venus in Libra

This planet-sign combination truly gives you an advantage when attracting all things Venusian: money, friendships, and admirers. Enjoying life's pleasures—fine food, art, fashion, and delightful conversations—makes your heart sing. Fairness and charm are your superpowers. Surrounding yourself with beauty and harmony is your motto, but getting overly attached to keeping the vibes peaceful at all costs makes for a superficial life as well as relationships. As long as you keep this tendency to idealize people and relationships in check, your life is smooth sailing.

Venus in Scorpio

Venus in Scorpio is the epitome of the Femme Fatale, so if you have this combination, your aura exudes sexuality. You're magnetic, seductive, and incredibly loyal. Superficial relationships bore you, as what you crave is to truly merge with someone at the deepest of levels. You're an all-or-nothing type of person, and those who you love know they can count on you. Reaching emotional depth and deep levels of intimacy is your specialty, but you should always keep tabs on this intensity morphing into either control or obsession.

Venus in Sagittarius

If you have Venus in Sagittarius, you're not only fun and exciting, you're a legit lover of life and a true seeker! Mental and physical exploration are your priorities and where you invest most of your time, money, and energy. A true wanderer, you ask life's most puzzling questions, feeling attraction to those, who, like you, are hungry to unlock the mysteries of the universe. Romantically, you need someone who is direct, philosophical, and always down for a good time.

Venus in Capricorn

Ambitious and goal-oriented, you are a practical person who might not date a lot, but once you find your match, you're not one to stray away easily. You take some time to warm up to people, and once you open up to them and care about them, you show it in ways that truly make an impact. Similarly, you're frugal with money, only spending on high-quality items, while also saving for either a rainy day or a long-term goal you hold close to your heart.

Venus in Aquarius

You have an unconventional streak when it comes to matters of the heart, approaching pleasure, love, and relationships differently. You experience emotions through a highly individualistic and detached lens, which some might misunderstand as coldness. For this reason, you prefer relating to people who are open-minded and highly self-confident. You're also deeply intellectual and need someone who is going to intellectually stimulate you. Some might say you avoid commitment, but the truth is that you're choosy and need a certain amount of freedom to roam through life at your own pace and desire.

Venus in Pisces

Congratulations, you have the strongest Venus sign there is, making you extremely sensitive, artistic, and a hopeless romantic. For you, it's not so much about falling in love with someone—it's more about being enamored with love itself! Being a tribe type of person, you have many options at your disposal but avoid getting yourself in too many commitments. After all, you're completely aware that your heart ebbs and flows, just like the ocean's waves. When you do commit, it's crucial to avoid getting lost in your partner's sense of identity.

YOUR VENUS CYCLE
One Year

Note: Your Venus probably won't be in this position within your chart. What this illustration seeks to convey is how your Venus cycle works. However, it does not include retrogrades, as each retrograde Venus is unique, bringing a different flavor each time.

On the following page are all the Venus-Venus activations you experience every single year, over about twelve to fourteen months. Unlike the Sun's activations, those of Venus are less predictable due to the retrograde of Venus, which happens every eighteen months, and lasts for about forty days. Your Venus activations are so important to take advantage of, as these are times when life gets sweet and the universe smiles at us. Even when life gets intense, you have Venus to fall back to, reminding you of the pleasures of life.

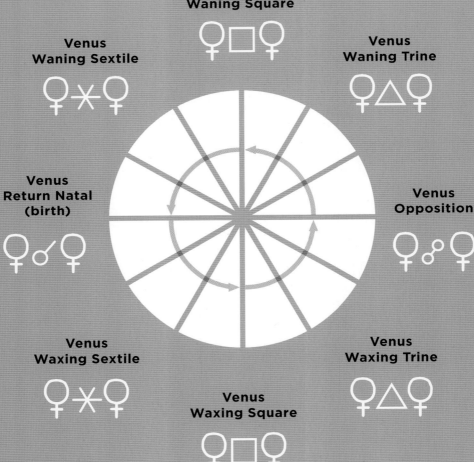

Venus
Waning Square

Venus
Waning Sextile

Venus
Waning Trine

Venus
Return Natal
(birth)

Venus
Opposition

Venus
Waxing Sextile

Venus
Waxing Square

Venus
Waxing Trine

To get even more specific dates regarding your current (or next) Venus activations, head to this page: www.naramon.com/written-in-your-stars. Then match the results with the text below.

Strategies for Harnessing Your Venus Returns
Timing: Once a year, lasting for about eight days
Arriving either one month before your birthday, on your birthday month, or even one month past your birthday, your Venus Return (which means Venus going to the same place it was when you were born) is a reinvigoration of your feminine side. It marks a new cycle, a reset during which you experience shifts concerning your approach to pleasure, love, relationships, and even money. Here are some tips:

1. Focus on relationships: You're feeling warm-hearted and with a stronger desire to connect, making this a good time to express your feelings for others: friends, partners, or even family.
2. Begin new connections: If you're ready to take a relationship to a new level of commitment, this would be a good time to make the move. We're talking about relationships of all kinds: romantic, business, and friendships.
3. Socialize: If you're looking for a good time to mingle and meet new people, this is a fabulous time to do so. Out of all Venus activations, your Venus Return amps up your charm, helping you feel seen and maybe even land new friendships and connections.
4. Go shopping: You will naturally desire to beautify yourself now, and this is one of the best times of the year to acquire new clothes, get a haircut, and even come up with a new look.
5. Focus on enjoying what you love: Take advantage of one of the best times of the year to embody your Venus sign (in the section above). For example, if you have Venus in Libra, go check out an art show; or if you have Venus in Sagittarius, plan to travel during this time.

Strategies for Harnessing Your Venus Sextiles
Timing: Twice a year, lasting for about eight days

Being one of the most positive planetary activations, your Venus Sextile brings a sense of easiness to your life, when things more likely than not work out as expected. Since the sextile is an aspect of opportunity, be open to see what or who comes into your life now. Here are some tips:

1. Take time off: Whether it's a day off, a weekend getaway, or a major trip, you're bound to have a great time now during these two time periods within the year. You might meet incredible people who ride the same wavelength as you.
2. Make moves on investments: Since Venus also rules money, this would be a good time to either make financial moves or purchase big-ticket items while Venus has your back.
3. Ask for a raise: If you know you deserve a raise and have been waiting for the right time to ask for it, choose one of the two times of the year during which you experience this Venus activation. While it is not a sure thing you will get it, the odds can be in your favor.
4. Make new friends: Venus represents social status, and yours is elevated during this time, bringing the perfect time to mingle within new social circles as you charm people away!

Strategies for Navigating Your Venus Squares
Timing: Twice a year, lasting for about eight days

In astrology, the square is an aspect of tension, when the transiting planet (Venus traveling in the sky) is clashing with the planet in your chart (your Venus). Luckily, this is one of the least volatile squares you can experience due to Venus being one of the easiest planets. Here are some tips:

1. Observe interactions within your relationships: This is one of those times when someone might ask you to compromise your points of view or give up your desires for the sake of making room for theirs. If possible, ask for more time, as you might regret saying yes later on.
2. Save your energy: You might feel tired for no reason or a little unmotivated at this time. Alternatively, you might want to rest and skip work but might realize you can't due to commitments you already made.

3. Avoid extravagant behaviors: It's not that experiencing pleasure is bad—but during these times, you might go overboard. Keep an eye on your spending, and your partying (drinking and over-eating).

4. Delay any big beauty treatments: Since Venus rules beauty and it is not in a friendly position to your natal Venus, it's best to leave any permanent aesthetic work (like tattoos, surgeries, or meaningful changes) for another time.

Strategies for Harnessing Your Venus Trines

Timing: Twice a year, lasting for about eight days

Like the Venus sextile, your Venus Trines are very positive in the sense that you're feeling more relaxed and at ease. Venus things (relationships, money, and pleasure) are bound to go well or as expected. However, to make the best of this activation, it is crucial to stay open to the possibilities that come your way. Here are some tips:

1. Be willing to connect: The people who come into your life at this time could prove to be helpful, even if that isn't obvious now. Say yes to meetings and social gatherings, and get to know people whose personality speaks to you.

2. Plan a date: Single or attached, this is a good time to romantically connect with someone at a deep level. The vibe between you will most likely flow as your desire to experience pleasure gets activated.

3. Take time for more rest and relaxation: If you're experiencing difficult activations or transits (like your Saturn Return, for example), Venus now provides you a window of easiness, kind of like a break from the intensity. If it's possible for you, this is a good time to plan a weekend getaway or even a vacation so you can unwind.

4. Seek inspiration: Since Venus is the planet that rules your five senses, this is a wonderful time to expose yourself to art, beauty, nature, and anything that will awaken a sense of awe within you. You can benefit the most if you're an artist, a writer, or other creative type.

Strategies for Navigating Your Venus Oppositions
Timing: Once a year, lasting for about eight days
Since the Venus Opposition happens only once a year, you might feel it stronger than the sextiles, squares, and oppositions. This is about finding a balance when it comes to dealing with all things Venus (pleasure, money, and relationships).

1. Manage sexual urges wisely: You may now crave attention from others and could go to great lengths to get it. Like, for example, hooking up with that tireless admirer, only to regret it later. Instead of looking for reassurance outside, develop it within by making art, hanging out with close friends, or pampering yourself.
2. Avoid negotiations: As the ruler of the zodiac sign Libra, Venus is the planet that oversees diplomacy and negotiations. During these eight days, transiting Venus is not in a friendly position to your natal Venus, meaning that you have the odds against you when it comes to the result.
3. Avoid scheduling important projects: More likely than not, you will feel uninspired to get stuff done now. All you want to do is have fun and enjoy life; If possible, delay any heavy work projects, especially if they have a creative component to them.
4. Delay key decision-making within relationships: If someone pops the question: "So . . . what are we?" during these eight days, try buying yourself some time before arriving at a conclusion. While it doesn't always happen, conflict can arise now—and while you should listen to the other person's point of view (which might be opposite to yours), you might have difficulty finding a middle ground.

Mars

Keywords
Action, Ambition, Courage, Sexuality, Passion,
Willpower, Drive, Conquest, Strength,
Impulsiveness, Survival Instinct, Assertiveness,
Anger, Rage, Machismo

Mars Archetypes
The Warrior, The Activator, The Motivator,
The Trainer, The Firefighter, The Hero,
Divine Masculine Archetype

The Astronomy of Mars

Like Venus, Mars is the other planet closest to us. You have most likely spotted Mars in the sky at some point due to its red brilliance, which derives from its oxidized iron composition turned to dust. A cold desert now, the red planet is one of the most explored in our solar system due to its proximity to Earth, but also because scientists believe Mars at some point hosted life. Like our blue planet, Mars has polar ice caps and shows signs of ancient lakes, deltas, and lakebeds that once emerged from its now-extinct volcanos.

Although Mars has a very thin atmosphere, it does not provide much protection from impacts by such objects as meteorites, asteroids, and comets. Mars has an impulsive type of weather, with occasional massive dust storms covering the entire planet for months at a time. As you can see, Mars is an inhospitable place, at least for us humans.

The Astrology of Mars

The ancient Romans named Mars after their god of agriculture, who eventually became the protector of their civilization, and, the god of war due to its reddish color reminiscent of blood. Like its atmosphere and weather, the effects of Mars are intense, ranging from defined and positive action to impulsive displays of anger and even rage.

Like Venus, Mars is also considered a "relationship planet," as it rules sexual drive, boundary setting, and how you defend yourself when life calls for it. Mars is the planet of masculine energy and that fire within fueling your desires and goals. Many think that, when it comes to love, relationships, and sex, we must only look at Venus. But the cosmic lovers go hand in hand: Venus rules sensuality (our ability to receive pleasure) while Mars rules sexuality (our ability to chase that pleasure). Venus is the planet that defines who you feel attracted to, but Mars is the planet that helps you chase it!

This is no coincidence, as Earth is sandwiched between Venus and Mars (the famous mythological lovers), speaking of the endless human journey toward finding a balance between feminine and masculine sides. In your birth chart, the placement of Mars speaks of your confidence levels, the way you assert yourself, and how you handle conflict.

Mars' Lower Vibration

Western society hasn't done a great job of integrating Mars energy, as openly expressed opposition can be widely criticized. As a result, some of us tend to repress it—but as we know from studying natural laws: energy can't die, it can only be transformed. Mars is the planet that teaches us that unprocessed anger festers deep inside of us, only to grow and be expressed later.

The other lower manifestation of Mars is extreme anger and aggression—either expressed by us or directed at us. If you are repressing your anger or finding it hard to defend yourself due to fear, you are not harnessing your Mars when it comes to setting boundaries. If, on the contrary, you blow up easily, angered at one thing or another, constantly reacting to things not going your way, you're allowing your masculine energy (Mars) to overpower your feminine energy (Venus).

The most extremely negative side of Mars is known as toxic masculinity and machismo (not necessarily gender-based), which is often displayed in news about shootings and other violent acts.

Embodying Mars' Higher Vibration

Since Mars is a tricky planet to master due to what it oversees, to help you understand how its highest vibration can manifest, think of a kung fu martial artist or perhaps a firefighter. What these two people have in common is the focused, organized, and positive expression of masculine energy. They're both highly trained and know when to wait and when to act!

You embody the highest vibration of your Mars energy when you act on your desires, even if you don't do it in a go-getter type of way—it's the act that counts! Even if you have Mars in a feminine (earth or water) sign, you're not waiting around to see if opportunity knocks at your door; you follow your bliss. Embodied masculine energy shows up as confidence in yourself regardless of your gender, sexual orientation, or appearance.

Another true Martian skill is being able to express your anger in constructive ways, which might involve waiting for the right time and space to do so. Even if you decide not to act on your anger, you make the effort to transmute this energy into a ritual, or exercise, or even yelling at the top of a mountain, conscious of not letting it fester deep inside of you.

Finding Your Mars Sign

If you don't know your Mars sign, you're in for a major epiphany. Why Mars and not other planets? Mars stuff feels intense, as it is the fuel that drives you. The astrological house where Mars is in your chart, specifically, is the area of life you more likely than not feel a little bit of an aversion to or that is the most in-your-face difficult.

Now, I invite you to think about the area of life that is harder for you to master. Next, enter it in this calculator www.naramon.com/birth-chart-calculator and find out how you handle sex, passion, anger, conflict, and drive.

Your Mars Sign, Explained

Mars in Aries

Aries is one of the strongest signs for Mars, making you a pioneer, a catalyst, and either a bit or very impatient. Direct and spontaneous, you are a master at initiating things and love giving birth to fresh ideas. For you, life is an exciting challenge to tackle, as you live in the moment, always searching for the next big thing. When someone wrongs you, you're quick to get angry—but you're just as quick when it comes to forgiving and forgetting. Action, sex, and exercise are crucial to your well-being.

Mars in Taurus

Let's be real—you take a while to make decisions, but once you do it, it's almost impossible to get you to change your mind. This gives you incredible endurance and staying power when it comes to achieving your goals. However, it can also make things difficult when embracing that change is not only an option but required. Instead of sexual, you are sensual, preferring slow and delicious movements instead of rushing through the process of connecting. You're also pretty serious about making money, as you're all about living a comfortable life.

Mars in Gemini

More likely than not, you're pretty restless, as this is the "monkey mind" planet-sign combination. Your intellect is quick and hungry for knowledge, so you most likely feed it by constantly reading, writing, and speaking—you're a master multitasker! But when you manage to stay focused on one project at a time without sending your energy in too many directions, you achieve incredible results. You have an incredible passion for and a special talent for words, but when you get angry, you might say things you later regret.

Mars in Cancer

If you have Mars in Cancer, your passion, drive, and even anger are very tied to your emotions. You feel your way through life, especially when it comes to chasing your goals and making your mark in the world. You're not into initiating fights, but you will do so if anyone from your family or soul-tribe is being attacked or taken advantage of. Otherwise, you're good at keeping your cool. However, you must always make sure anger isn't festering, as it could easily turn into passive-aggressiveness.

Mars in Leo

Fiery and passionate, you lead with your heart and have a strong sense of confidence. You're ambitious and yearn to create a life of meaning for yourself that goes beyond just "being successful." When it comes to relationships, you're magnetic, attracting the object of your desire with ease and grace. You do have a serious sexual appetite and require the same loyalty you offer to those you love that you give in return. However, when you get upset, sparks fly, and you most likely struggle with letting go of anger, needing movement as a form of release.

Mars in Virgo

You are a productive individual with a special talent for analyzing, organizing, and getting things done. A multitasker but still a perfectionist, you get satisfaction from reaching high levels of productivity; however, you must always stay conscious of overworking yourself, which can be detrimental to your sense of well-being. When it comes to sex and relationships, you find happiness whenever you're able to flow with the energy at play, instead of noticing everything that could at some point go wrong.

Mars in Libra

You struggle with making decisions, weighing all the options at your disposal before making a move. This is especially true when it comes to relationships, as you're very (if not extremely) careful when dealing with others. Diplomacy and tact are some of the qualities that some of those around you admire, as very few can match your patience whenever dealing with complicated situations or scenarios. To keep the harmony and peace, however, you are one to easily sweep things under the rug, which can eventually create bigger issues.

Mars in Scorpio

Scorpio is one of the strongest signs for Mars, giving you an incredible sense of ambition, willpower, and sexual stamina. On the outside, you're cool and collected, but on the inside, you're always confronted with a strong desire to achieve something difficult—or even impossible! You love putting yourself through tests, always competing with others and even yourself. Unraveling people's motives, drives, and desires is your specialty and one you perform naturally and with precise secrecy. However, without enough awareness, this unique gift can easily entangle you in emotionally manipulative scenarios.

Mars in Sagittarius

Fun, warm, and playful, you're a true free spirit with an incredible hunger to experience life in all its splendor. We can always find you running around from one gathering to the next, spreading joyful vibes but also your philosophical worldviews that seek to inspire deep thinking. Whenever dealing with serious or intense situations, your desire to escape kicks in, as your endless optimism prefers avoiding emotionally charged scenarios. When it comes to relationships, you're hard to pin down as you crave the freedom to explore all the available options.

Mars in Capricorn

You're in luck! Capricorn is the most prominent zodiac sign for the red planet, elevating your masculine energy to an orderly, focused, and productive expression. "Anything is possible" is not only your mantra but truly the way you live your life, always achieving goals and reaching places few would even dare to explore. Your success is not necessarily "written in your stars"; you have gained it by embodying a disciplined, steady, and strategic approach toward your goals. As a lover, you're skillful and agile but also down to earth.

Mars in Aquarius

Having the planet of energy and drive in the most original zodiac sign gives you a cool, controlled, and puzzling demeanor. Just when people think they've figured you out, here you come with some extraordinary idea about life or some otherworldly theme-sparking intellectual conversation. For you, love and relationships must be fun, dynamic, and never restrictive; freedom is a value you defend, believe in, and stick to! You're pretty set in your beliefs, and it would take a village to get you to change your mind.

Mars in Pisces

Having the planet of action in the oceanic sign of Pisces feels like trying to run while being in an immense pool. This means you have a soft demeanor in your goal-setting and goal-chasing, often employing more unusual tactics than most to get to the same destination. A true believer in destiny, you're more into letting the universe take the reins instead of trying to control your life. People love your flowy, chameleon-like ability to shift and adapt. But when you resolve that you truly desire something, especially concerning relationships, being more direct is your way to get what or who you want.

YOUR MARS CYCLE
Two Years

Note: Your Mars probably won't be in this position within your chart. What this illustration seeks to convey is how your Mars cycle works. However, it does not include retrogrades, as each retrograde of Mars is unique, bringing a different flavor each time.

On page 196 are all the Mars-Mars activations you experience throughout twenty-four to twenty-six months. Due to Mars overseeing personal energy and drive, these activations are very noticeable within our sense of vitality, ambition, and desire. Unlike the Sun's activations, those of Mars are less predictable due to its retrogrades, which happen every twenty-six months for eight to eleven weeks. Since Mars is the first planet beyond Earth in our solar system, it only goes retrograde every twenty-six months for about two to two-and-a-half months.

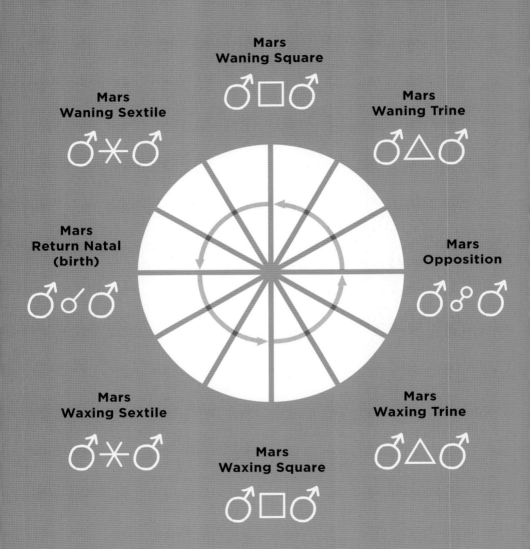

To get even more specific dates regarding your current (or next) Mars activations, head to this page: www.naramon.com/written-in-your-stars. Then match the results with the text below.

Strategies for Harnessing Your Mars Returns

Timing: Two to two-and-a-half years, lasting for about fourteen days

Your Mars Return (which means Mars going to the same place it was when you were born) is a reinvigoration of your masculine side. This bi-yearly activation is important to pay attention to, as it represents a massive reset of not only your drive and ambition but also your most primal desires! During this time, your body receives a huge boost of energy, bringing some of the most action-packed days of your personal Mars cycle. Here are some tips:

1. Move your body: You will feel extra energy running through you, requiring release via strenuous movement, exercise, or heavy lifting work. If you are not someone who works out, you should now. If you are already an active person, you might be required to amp it up even more.

2. Avoid snapping at other people: You may now feel triggered—either for a really good reason or for no reason at all. Spending time alone might be ideal now, as starting a fight will only magnify the inner tension you now feel. This is especially true if you have Mars in a fixed sign (Taurus, Leo, Scorpio, or Aquarius).

3. Find a positive outlet: On the positive side, this can be a fantastic time to begin new things, as you have a lot more energy at your disposal. Passion projects that require long hours of work and focus can be especially rewarding at this time.

4. Embrace sexual experimentation: In mythology, Mars is known as the God of Sex, so this is your moment to find release via orgasm and, if you're so inclined, to stretch your boundaries.

5. Redirect anger: Go for a brisk walk, or write a letter and burn it, but do not repress your feelings, as they will come back later on, most likely during your Mars Square or Mars Opposition.

Strategies for Harnessing Your Mars Sextiles

Timing: Once a year, lasting for about fourteen days

Being one of the two most positive Mars-Mars activations you experience within the two-year Mars cycle, your Mars Sextile is something you want to make the best of. You feel a surge of energy, but it is more subtle, which means that without purposely harnessing it, you might not even feel its effect too much besides feeling a type of influence that feels pleasant. Here are some tips:

1. Tackle difficult tasks: You're feeling confident in your abilities now and can excel at any type of interaction that involves expressing your will. Business meetings, negotiations, or even difficult conversations planned now are likely to go well.
2. Get stuff done: This is one of the best planetary activations for pulling out your to-do list and crossing items off, especially those that seem more important or that you would like to get ahead on.
3. Seek newness in your life: If there is something that Mars loves it is action! Harness these days by meeting new people, traveling to new places, and enjoying new vistas.
4. Embrace teamwork: Your ideas are more influential now, making this a great time to collaborate with others toward a shared goal. You're also more open to listening to other people's opinions and more apt to create win-win scenarios and solutions.

Strategies for Navigating Your Mars Squares

Timing: Once a year, lasting for about fourteen days

This is one of the two times within the two-year Mars cycle when Mars traveling in the sky will challenge your natal Mars, bringing a few days of triggering energy. There is no way to sugarcoat it, your Mars Square is one to approach with care and great awareness. Expect this to be easier said than done if your Mars is either in a fire sign (Aries, Leo, or Sagittarius) or in aspect to your Sun, Moon, or Rising Sign. Here are some tips:

1. Avoid impulsivity: In a moment of irritability, impatience, or anger, you might suddenly act in unexpected ways, leaving others perplexed. Even if you feel like you can get away with it, you most likely can't and might even gain a few enemies along this process.

2. Rethink unnecessary risks: Mars is the planet of accidents, making the days surrounding this activation less than ideal for jumping off a plane, riding your bike without a helmet, testing your limits while working out, or any other activity that could harm you. Be specifically careful if you are also having a Uranus activation (see the Uranus section).

3. Delay important discussions: If you have important decisions to make, bold moves to perform, or delicate discussions to have, try delaying them. If you cannot, try keeping a low profile or be very strategic about what you say or do.

4. Nurture your body and system: Some people get sick during this Mars activation. Protect yourself by allowing time for extra sleep, taking vitamins, and planning light work and workout schedules.

Strategies for Harnessing Your Mars Trines
Timing: Once a year, lasting for about fourteen days

Your Mars Trine is one you want to keep tabs on because it brings some of your most productive and powerful days of the year. You can think of Mars traveling in the sky supporting, fueling, and feeding your natal Mars with a boost of can-do energy. Obviously, the worst thing you could do now is waste this opportunity by not making the best of the extra amps building up inside of you. Here are some tips:

1. Begin something new: Whatever you start now has the chance of being successful over time, making this a powerful time to charge ahead on an important goal. If possible, check the current lunar cycle and make your move right after the next New Moon.

2. Focus on solo projects: With the right focus, you could get more done than what you normally produce during the past two months. Your body is in sync with your mind, giving you an incredible amount of stamina to be and stay productive.

3. Express your masculine side: Regardless of the nature of your endeavor, this is one of those times when acting assertively will impress others. Your aura is magnetic, giving you the confidence needed to accomplish hard-to-get things.

4. Explore sexual connections: Since your magnetism is turned on, this would be a good time to have sex with someone new or have more sex with an existing partner. You are clear about expressing what you want, which facilitates the exchange of pleasure.

Strategies for Navigating Your Mars Oppositions
Timing: Once every two years, lasting for about fourteen days
The Mars Opposition can be tricky, but with the right attitude, it can help you learn the correct way to assert yourself. Because, in the end, paying attention to the effects of certain cycles can help us weave the information, zooming into why certain stories repeat again and again. This is especially true when it comes to the Mars Opposition, as it is the type of energy that ignites the most primal of all feelings and desires. Here are some tips:

1. Asset yourself positively: You are feeling fired up and in need of showing people what you've accomplished and what you're made of. Great! Go ahead and show off a little, but do so without throwing any other people under the bus, as that could backfire. This is not about repressing your desires—it's more about making your mark without coming off as egotistical.
2. Reflect on your goals: While feeling this desire for success, you might set on a quest to chase something just to have it or for the sake of competing with an enemy or rival. Chase what's truly on *your* agenda and not someone else's.
3. Find balance in relationships: Alternatively, you might have someone challenge your views, values, or work now. Replace any desire to respond in a passive-aggressive manner; instead, be direct and open about the situation at hand.
4. Stay out of drama: People might try to involve you in tricky situations with the intent of getting you "on their side." You might want to carefully excuse yourself from the situation at hand as getting involved could bring negative consequences later.

CONCLUSION

You have arrived at the end of this book—congratulations! But your dance with the planets and their archetypes is just beginning. Using this book as a companion to your personal evolution, you will become aware of your relationship with each of the planets in our solar system. The best part is that you get to choose how that relationship develops with the passage of time. Ancient wisdom has always affirmed that living in attunement with the cycles of nature is the best way of experiencing life. The bliss that comes from living with the cycles of yourself, your astral DNA, is incomparable to anything else you can possibly experience as a human.

My wish is that this book holds your hand in that awakening process, empowering you to live life on your own terms in a constant state of awe, flow, magic, and evolution.

With stellar gratitude,
Narayana

ASTROLOGICAL SYMBOLS

Planets

 Jupiter

 Saturn

 Chiron

 Uranus

 Neptune

 Pluto

Lunar Nodes

 Sun

 Moon

 Mercury

 Venus

 Mars

Zodiac Signs

 Aries

 Taurus

 Gemini

 Cancer

 Leo

 Virgo

 Libra

 Scorpio

 Sagittarius

 Capricorn

 Aquarius

 Pisces

Aspects

 Conjunction

 Opposition

 Square

 Trine

 Sextile

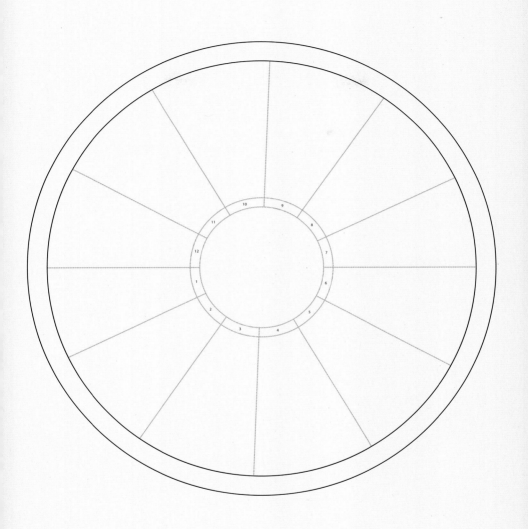

Use this blank chart to help you
remember where your planets and
zodiac signs are—get creative!

ABOUT THE AUTHOR

Narayana Montúfar is an astrologer, writer, artist, Akashic Records reader, and the author of *Moon Signs: Unlock Your Inner Luminary Power*. With thirteen years of experience in the spiritual industry, she has accumulated extensive knowledge that has landed her features in multiple lifestyle publications worldwide.

Narayana was featured as one of Medium.com's *Authority Magazine*'s "2020 Strong Female Leaders," *Destig* magazine's "Top Artists to Collect in 2020," and one of *Vogue India*'s "13 Astrologers to Follow on Instagram Now" in 2020. In her private astrology practice, Narayana's holistic approach seeks to create a positive impact by directing each one of her clients toward their unique soul path and life purpose.

ACKNOWLEDGMENTS

Written in Your Stars is dedicated to the four extraordinary men in my life, whose presence has illuminated the beauty and strength of the Divine Masculine.

To the three fathers, protectors, and guides who left this dimension too soon but continue to shape my life through the loving space the Akasha provides for my healing and evolution.

To my grandfather, Jorge Montúfar Araujo (Tito), my guardian angel and fierce protector across lifetimes: My love for you transcends dimensions.

To my biological father, Jorge Alberto Ávila, who returned through the Reiki portal to remind me that healing is possible when I embrace the spiritual path as my sanctuary.

To my stepdad, Gerardo Niño de Rivera, who loved me unconditionally and taught me that the greatest answer to life's challenges is to surrender to love.

To my forever soul companion, Alex Drossler, for fifteen years of globe-trotting adventures, a decade of blissful marriage, and your unwavering support of my dreams.

Written in Your Stars would not exist without the guidance of my angels, spirit guides, and star family, who inspire me to trust in myself and the divine purpose of my work.

And to you, the reader: Thank you from the bottom of my heart.

With stellar gratitude,
Narayana

INDEX